THE COMPLEAT IMBIBER 8

They are fine, strapping young ladies, suggesting appropriately that good looks are not incompatible with good nourishment. Their flesh is a slightly sunburnt off-white, their nipples are as unmarked as the Beaverbrook Press could wish . . . *Nicholas Taylor, page* 90

The Compleat

Imbiber 8

AN ENTERTAINMENT — EDITED

BY Cyril Ray AND DESIGNED

BY Charles Hasler

COLLINS — LONDON — 1965

Harveys of Bristol,
who sponsor the eighth issue of *The Compleat Imbiber*, offer this
compendium of entertainment and information to all amateurs
of wine and good living.
The Compleat Imbiber, which was first published in 1956, has
been edited since its inception by Cyril Ray

The text of this book is set in 11pt Monotype Scotch Roman.
Printed and bound in Great Britain at Collins Clear-Type Press,
Glasgow

Published by COLLINS
14 St James's Place, London S.W.1

Contents

Acknowledgments

Especial thanks are due to the editor of *The Architectural Review* for making available text and illustrations of the article on the Black Friar and for his prompt and understanding collaboration in the centenary article on the Café Royal grill room: thanks are also due to the two photographers, Mr H. de Burgh Galwey and Mr Eric de Maré, respectively, as well as to the author, and to Mr Charles Forte and Mr Mervyn Cherrington for their help in making the Café Royal photographs possible. The articles by Mr Alan Brien and Mrs Elizabeth David first appeared in *The Spectator*, to the editor of which I am obliged, as I am to the management of the National Magazine Co, Ltd, for permission to reproduce Mr Arnold Schwarzman's illustrations to *The Great Carp Ferdinand*, which was first published in *Good Housekeeping*. Dr Otto Loeb kindly lent the old Glyndebourne wine-lists to illustrate his own article, for which I am grateful, as I am to the editor of *Vintage* for permission to reprint Dr Dickerson's and Professor Orr's articles. Mr Michael Broadbent's article on tasting was first published in the *Wine and Spirit Trade Record*.

My colleague Charles Hasler, designer of this book, thanks the United States Information Service, the West Virginia Pulp & Paper Co, the Parker Gallery, Arthur Guinness Sons & Co, Ltd, the Radio Times Hulton Picture Library, and Mr Andrew Block. He also salutes the memory of George Cruikshank, Honoré Daumier, Gustave Doré, P. Frenzeny, T. M. Cleland, Paul Sandby, Eugène Delacroix, Thomas Rowlandson, Tischbein, Winart, Kip and the unknown artist of the postcards reproduced on pages 171 and 172.

                                                C.R.

Introduction

BY CYRIL RAY

INE is grown in pleasant places, and a writer about wine may well be grateful. Much of *Compleat Imbiber No. 8* was planned in Siena, where I lived for a couple of months last winter, working at the Wine Museum there on a book about Italian wines, and making sorties into the Chianti country round about. And, at other times, to have to visit Bordeaux, or the Moselle villages, or the Alpine slopes of the Alto Adige, where the Italian rieslings and traminers come from, all in the course of duty, is no hardship.

I have an especial affection for the brandy capital, where I have idled away some of my pleasant duty visits, lapped in the quietness of a sleepy country town. For Cognac is small indeed for a town with so resounding a name—as populous as Buxton, say, or Bury St. Edmunds: a quiet grey place in a quiet green landscape.

This is where the Sud-ouest begins. Cognac is the northernmost outpost of the stamping-ground of the greatest French rugby-footballers, who play the game (if that is the appropriate phrase) with Gascon vehemence. Its own team is made up of tigers lured from Lourdes, or poached from Pau, with the offers of jobs in the distilleries or the counting-houses of Martell or of Hennessy.

There are other forms of wild life, too, that give the little town an air of the south. So that although it can be cool here, of an autumn evening, there are screens on the windows against local mosquitoes that are as dashing as d'Artagnan's *mousquetaires* (though d'Artagnan himself came from farther south still, from Armagnac, where the other great brandy is made). And the tiled roofs, sooted with brandy fumes, have the shallow pitch of the south.

In the long summer days the Charente seems hardly to flow, more lake than river, reflecting as sharply as a picture-postcard the grey walls and green willows; in the fields the small greeny-gold grapes ripen that will produce the thin, harsh wine from which new cognac is made. And in the huge sheds—there is no underground cellaring in Cognac any more than there is in Jerez —the spirit matures in its casks of Limousin and Troncey oak, taking on colour from the wood, waiting to be blended with its elder brothers and to burgeon into a modest three-star, a social-climbing V S O P, or perhaps even one of those aristocratic *marques* that cost twelve shillings a glass and more at the Coq d'Or, the café-brasserie in the tiny town's tiny central square, where the equestrian figure of Cognac's most illustrious son, François I, prances eternally in bronze. There are more than a hundred cognacs on the list at the Coq d'Or, every one of them a cut above three-star, along with a recommendation to try the aperitif of the region, *pineau des Charentes*, which is grape-juice, the fermentation of which has been checked by added brandy, as with the ratafia of Champagne, and to my taste too rich a drink for before dinner.

There is no immediately local table wine: it is all made into brandy, and would not be very nice if it weren't. But the Cognac country lies between the Loire and the Blayais, and the whites of the one and the reds of the other are near enough to be regional. They wash down steaks grilled over vine branches, tunny from the Atlantic (cooked, at one of the little local restaurants, in a Chartreuse sauce), oysters and clams and mussels from the beds at Arcachon or Marennes, not far away, the oysters eaten, as is the custom in these parts, with a hot grilled sausage in the side —first an oyster, then a bite at the sausage.

This is the country that gives its name to the Charentais melon, slices of which, with oysters or clams, are always served with the local hors d'œuvre. I ate those, and pâté, too, and a fat little pigeon in red wine, lunching out at the Cognac restaurant called Robinson—named after Crusoe, I think, as the French like to name their rusticities, for it is on an island in the river—and sat afterwards with my cognac cradled in my hand, sniffing from it the essence of the sunshine that for centuries of summers has blessed the trees that shaded me, the ripening vineyards on the opposite bank, the river at my feet. How soothing to the sensibilities to sip a brandy old enough to be your father!

At the Wrong End of the Wine List

BY KATHARINE WHITEHORN

HENEVER I go to tastings I find myself making two little marks against the red wines which mean nothing, fortunately, to anyone looking over my shoulder: S. and I.F. S. is supposed to represent all bland, mild, soft wines, and I.F. all the sharper, stronger tastes; and they stand for Soap and Iron Filings. I have never been able to find a way of describing good qualities with the simple accuracy with which one can pin down bad ones; so the two categories (into which one can divide all red wines) have to be represented by their dregs. And I am inclined to think that your real turning-point as a wine-drinker is the moment when you realise with astonishment that there *are* any positively attractive qualities to wine—fruitiness, or a heavenly smell or whatever— instead of just a welcome lack of the bad qualities you know so well. It is the moment when you realise that there are other things for a wine to be than just *not* too sweet, too muddy, too expensive or too warm that the noble rot sets in: from that point there is nothing between you and château-bottled Château Margaux and the hock they drink in heaven.

But down among the iron filings one can have a lot of fun, and that, I imagine, is where most of us began—not rolling around in old college port like Evelyn Waugh and Raymond Postgate.* Me, I have always liked just *any* old kind of wine— in fact it is extremely sad for me that there are no winos in Britain. I would love to be one, but all the people who acquire divine vision and cirrhosis of the liver in this country do it on whisky or meths or gin, and you cannot be a wino all by yourself. Other countries do better: Omar Khayyám, the wino's

* See these two authors' contributions to *Compleat Imbiber 6* and *Compleat Imbiber 1*, respectively. Editor.

wino, had it in a nutshell. He didn't say that lately, by the Tavern Door agape, Came stealing through the Dusk an Angel Shape, Bearing a vessel on his Shoulder; and He bid me taste of it; and 'twas a 1953er Schloss Vollrads Trockenbeerenauslese. What the man said was *grape*.

Though, come to think of it, even being made of grape puts a wine several rungs up from the bottom of the ladder—look at all those homely unspoiled do-it-yourself country wines that are mainly responsible for the drift to the towns. My mother did one out of elderberries, I remember, which we used to drink sitting across the kitchen table from each other like a couple of Hogarthian hags; it cost about one and fourpence a bottle, a fact of which we found it necessary to remind ourselves before every gulp. And there were some appalling specimens (I pick my words) that were submitted in medicine bottles to the *Farmer's Weekly* Home Made Wine competition back in 1957, the runners-up being sold off at a bob a time to the staff of Hulton Press. Just what the proportions of wurzels, whortleberries, sukebind, beestings and the sump water of disused tractors were, that we absorbed, I do not remember; I can only recall one of the vilest hangovers ever, and the sticky little bottles on the window-sills reminding one of it for weeks afterwards.

Obviously, if you make a wine yourself, you can forgive it a lot (the same is true of children). One of the nastiest wines I ever came across I helped to make myself: it was a thin rosé of the Côte d'Azur. They still picked their grapes on this sea-facing slope, but the price of villas being what it was, their hearts were no longer in it. About the only thing that wasn't: it was compounded mainly of bad red grapes, bad white grapes, dead snails and Ambre Solaire; and the fact that even they charged even us only 100 old francs a bottle is a measure of just how awful it was.

But the *vendange* was fun. In a big local gaggle under the hot sun we wove to and fro in a desultory way until it was time for the lunch that was our reward: a huge seething *bouillabaisse* cooked in the open on the beach. My husband, who had eaten till the crabs came out of his ears the day before, simply couldn't face it again, and invented an upset stomach; he was not (he carefully explained) getting out of the work but out of the belly-bursting reward. It was a mistake. In Provence they don't just say, 'Ah, an upset stomach' and let it go at that; and he had well-wishers calling with suggestions, potions and a barrage of extremely personal questions for three days. Those of us who finished the day's picking in the hot sun had, to my mind, the best of it, in spite of undergoing the real hardship of the labouring classes—featuring as Jolly Peasants in somebody else's colour movie.

All this, however, was long after we had realised that even cheap wines don't have to taste quite as bad as that. In the beginning it would hardly even be true to say we started at the wrong end of the wine list—we started at the bottom of the menu, where it said 'Red, 2s. a glass'—This price must have represented a profit of about two hundred and fifty per cent on the muck concerned but this I only realised when I got to the stage of having my own tiny little flat, my own eensy-weensy gas stove, overdraft and corkscrew (with tin-opener attachment) and started getting wine in by the bottle. It was mostly Spanish Burgundy (S) or Algerian (I.F.); and the big break-through happened with a blackish Chianti that came in plain covers, no straw. It had a lot of things to recommend it, like not being Spanish, and costing only 5s. 9d. a bottle; and knowing it was cheaper without the straw gave one an unwarrantable feeling of expertise. I suppose I offered it once a week for more than a year before someone put me off it for life with a single remark.

'Just red ink, I'm afraid,' I said, pouring gaily.

'I *knew* you'd say that!' my guest burst out, 'You *absolutely always do!*'

Even down at that level, it seems, it is not the wine you serve but the chat you serve with it that puts them off. Everyone smiles at phrases like 'a naïve domestic Burgundy' and 'a gay, unself-conscious Liebfraumilch,' but the hearty evasions of the uninitiated are just as bad: rotgut, vinegar, gnat's pee; battery acid, factory-bottled; snake-bite medicine; not a drop is sold till it's two days old, and—Oh God, oh Montecassino—'the jolly old *vino!*'

I suppose this last is so inescapable just because more British people have drunk more bad wine with pleasure in Italy than anywhere else. I know I have. The summer *Picture Post* folded, two of its lost sheep went abroad, to become united on the severance pay; we wandered round Europe in the warm weather, knowing that the lower our standard of living the longer we could stay away. That meant one meal a day maximum, the rest being picnics of bread and sausage and the kind of wine that doesn't even come out of bottles, but out of a thing like an oil drum at the back of the shop. The trouble was, really, that it *was* so cheap: there seemed no reason not to buy a litre a meal, which we would consume with our picnic on the ramparts of Porto Venere and then fall asleep. These ramparts, like the rocks on the beach, are hard, impressive and nowhere flat, and we would wake every day in agony, hobbling about the town in a way that must have made the locals think it was our mutual interest in arthritis that drew us together. Even the disastrous wine, however, was preferable to what happened the day we left. The people who had been renting us their family sitting-room at only about twice what the Ritz would have charged had an attack of conscience and offered us a farewell drink. Our national drink, they thought: neat gin; out of large glasses; at ten in the morning. Could they not, we felt, as we gulped our way to the boat —could they not have been content to rob us, without poisoning us as well?

One does not think of America as a wine country, but they make it, all right, and sometimes in a rash moment one drinks it. I remember once when I was camping with a friend in North Carolina we bought a bottle of wine in a supermarket for 69 cents which is not (apparently) enough. After one sip we put it aside as undrinkable, and concentrated on eating our dinner in the warm spring evening. Except that that particular evening it wasn't warm at all: maybe there was some misunderstanding about dates, maybe they thought it was a Federal spring and they folks warnt goin' to have no truck with it. Whatever the reason it froze hard: the peach trees froze; we froze; and I suppose the fact that that disgusting liquid *didn't* freeze proves that it must have had *some* alcohol in it. We moved the sleeping-bags into the car, smoked, did exercises, breathed hard: there was no getting away from the fact that it was going to be a bitter night. A drunken Negro asked us what on earth we were doing there, and we resented not his intrusion but the fact that we had to wind down the window for five whole seconds to tell him.

There was nothing for it but to down the whole bottle of wine to keep from perishing. It felt like drinking a whole bottle of cough mixture at one go like a child doing it for a dare; like mariners moistening their lips with the sweat and blood of brother (or at any rate other) mariners. But we did it. Aubrey Menen was told that if he became a Hindu and purified himself by drinking a beaker of cow's urine he would inherit his father's wealth; he refused, and was reproved by his father with the words: 'My boy, if that's the worst thing you ever have to do for money, you'll be lucky'. I suppose a girl could say there are worse things to do to keep warm than drinking such stuff; but it didn't seem so at the time. We tottered out in the morning, frozen blue but surviving; the Negro reappeared and asked us back to his mother's for coffee and hot cakes; the sun shone. All the same, we reckoned that next time we would not buy the 69c wine, but go for the 72c and damn the expense.

Looking back, it all seems so simple. You bought not hock or Moselle, claret or burgundy, a good year or a bad: you just bought wine. We have passed the great divide now, thanks largely to my sharing an office with Cyril Ray, first at the *Spectator* and now at *The Observer*, and we strive ever upwards; but by God the going is rough. You buy a good named claret, and drink it five years too soon. You get the wine right and the year right and ask your wine friend when to open it; he says "Just before the meal,"—and you don't realise he still means you should decant it. A chum brings a bottle of Graves to hospital, and you know Graves is a white wine, so in a lordly way you ask the nurses to bung it in the fridge—if you'd never heard of Graves you'd have had a look at it first and seen that it was a red Graves. Your brother teaches your parents to warm the wine—so you have to teach them not to roast it like a chestnut in the ashes. The more fine qualities a wine has, it seems, the easier it is to wreck them in some way; one longs for simple indestructible *vin rouge*, to which nothing you can do or not do makes the slightest difference.

Even when you get it right, the mechanics of the thing can floor you. The other evening I went down to the people in the flat below to decant a bottle of good claret that had been left in their warm kitchen two days before. I had a candle and a decanter, the wine was in its basket, I had a corkscrew . . . a corkscrew! One of those 'simplified' jobs that you use because once you have one of them in the house the ordinary corkscrews for some reason won't work either; and it went in crooked, SSE. I tried again. Again crooked, but this time NNW. The third time, I found I had bored a small tunnel in the cork through which, amid a shower of cork and much rude laughter, I finally decanted the wine. A fine thing, I thought, when you know what wine, what year, what temperature and when to open it—and you can't get the goddam cork out of the bottle.

I suppose we shall soldier on; the trouble is, we now like decent wine. But it has its limitations. The other evening I was entertaining an old friend, and to celebrate the occasion suggested that we open a good bottle of claret. He gave it as his opinion that all this wine stuff was a lot of rot; and that wasn't the only tiresome thing he said that evening, not by a long chalk. Finally it got to the point where I threw a glass of wine at him, a thing I haven't done since I was married (though if you do throw wine once you are married, you are at least in a position to lend the victim a shirt). It was plonk, of course: after his disparaging remarks we had let the claret alone. But what I can't help wondering is whether I would have thrown it if it *had* been Pontet Canet 1937? And if not, does not that go to show that there is some of the fine dash of impetuous youth that you lose when you start trying too hard about wine? Well, maybe not; maybe all it proves is that in every properly conducted household there should be grand wine, swigging wine, cooking wine and throwing wine, to be judiciously selected as the occasion requires.

They Call it Hospitality

BY BERNARD LEVIN

OR many years now, I have been collecting material for a definitive study of the 'perks' obtainable, in the course of his employment, by a journalist of reasonably acquisitive instincts and a proper blend of integrity and common sense. In the final work there will, you may be sure, be an account of how I come to be the proud possessor of a magnificent and absolutely authentic replica of the carpet-bag taken round the world in eighty days by Phineas Fogg, as played by Mr David Niven in Mike Todd's film of the same name.

There will also be learned discussions, possible in Appendices, of such matters as the statistical differences between the contents of journalists' waste-paper baskets and those of other people, and to what extent these differences are accounted for by the presence, in the average journalist's discard-pile, of materials (such as diaries, notebooks, pencils, brochures, ashtrays, paper-knives, calendars, photographs and publishers' reminders) that are popularly supposed, by Public Relations Officers, to be a productive way of spending their clients' money.

This monograph, which it is already clear to me will be the study of a lifetime, will not be ready for many years. Meanwhile, however, I am prepared, from time to time, to publish certain more or less self-contained sections as 'Work in Progress', and just such a chapter, under the heading 'Food and drink for consumption on the premises' (that is, as opposed to the bottles of Scotch television reporters get from Mr Lew Grade at Christmas) has just been completed. A condensed version of it follows.

Any journalist whose work includes, to any considerable extent, television and radio broadcasting, will be familiar with what is known to the broadcasting authorities, for some laughably inadequate reason, as 'hospitality.' But only those who have spent as much time as I have, in a properly scientific frame of mind, examining and comparing the practice in this field of the different companies, can know the many subtle differences between the provision made for its performers by, say, the BBC, and that laid on by, say, Rediffusion.

The BBC, which really demands a separate study to itself, works, as you would expect, on a hierarchical or stratified principle. If you have lunch with the very highest echelons of the Corporation at the Studios (I am, of course, excluding the whole field of being taken out to a restaurant by executives or producers) you can eat extremely well, though even in those rarefied regions the menu appears to have been arranged by the repulsive 'J.B.', who knows of nothing but Dover sole and Liebfraumlich. But at any rate a real meal, consisting of food and drink that would be recognised as such elsewhere, can be obtained. (There are other, stranger, provisions made; though it is perfectly true, I can no longer find anybody to believe that I once took a shower in the BBC office of the late Cecil McGivern.)

At the next level, you come to the provision made in certain backwaters of sound radio, and in certain frontwaters of television, for a hot meal from the BBC kitchens served in somebody's office before the programme. The food here consists usually of chicken that would be refused indignantly as tasteless by a cannibal broiler-fowl, accompanied by peas that are clearly the lineal descendants of Napoleon's whiff of grapeshot, preceded by grapefruit of an acidity that necessitates its being served by a waitress wearing asbestos gloves, followed by a compote of the contents of five different tins, no two of which go together in any way, the whole being washed down by claret served so cold that I am ready to swear that I have on occasion cut my lip on the ice formed on the surface.

One step further down at the BBC, and you enter the regions where food and drink cease entirely to resemble anything met with anywhere else in the world, or even in television. Here, everything is based on the veal-and-ham pie, which comes in squares one inch thick, with half an egg showing, and is met with absolutely nowhere else—a fact which will be less surprising to those who have tasted it than to those who have not. This is accompanied by potato-salad, doused in bottled imitation ' salad-cream,' beetroot, and cream crackers.

Accompanying this stuff there is rarely so much as a doctored Algerian claret; hard liquor only is served, presumably on the grounds that only a stomach fortified by a substantial lining of neat Scotch will tolerate such fare without summarily ejecting it. The ice, however, has long since run out, and the gin is served warm; my suggestion that they should leave the tonic in whatever sub-arctic spot they find for the red wine at the higher level is consistently ignored.

It is when we follow our Virgil into the lowest region of all, however, that the feeling of having strayed into a nightmare grows overwhelming. Programme after programme in which I have taken part has attempted to nourish me before the performance on potato crisps and sandwiches so unutterably vile, so immeasurably unfit for human consumption, so absolutely unspeakably disgusting, that I have on occasion fallen upon the peanuts (which, under the provisions of some immutable law, are invariably served stale) and eaten half a pound of them.

Oddly enough, at this level the drink gets a good deal better. The bar run by the admirable Mrs Reynolds for the performers in *That Was the Week That Was* and subsequently for *Not So Much a Programme, More a Way of Life* included a perfectly drinkable Chablis, gin with ice in it, Worthington, and even brandy (a substance otherwise utterly unknown anywhere in any broadcasting organisation).

By comparison with the BBC, the commercial companies are simple in their catering arrangements. At Granada, for instance, you can't get any liquor at all. It is said that this goes back to an episode some years ago, when a celebrated jazz-band arrived at the studio for a performance, were supplied with a bottle of Scotch apiece, and got so high that their perfomance very nearly killed all sales of their records for ever. Coffee is supplied, though, and it is the one company that serves the milk and the coffee separately, each in its own vacuum-flask. But they fall down badly on the sandwiches; repulsive little crustless triangles filled with ham that never came off any pig I have ever met, or even heard of.

At Rediffusion you can drink yourself unconscious if you have a mind to, and with some of Rediffusion's programmes you certainly do have a mind to. But the only time I ever had a proper sit-down meal there it was an almost exact replica of the BBC's Grade II (where do they grow those melons that taste of nothing but the morello cherry?), though the wine was a bit better.

All in all, you don't eat or drink well if you do so at the expense of broadcasting authorities in this country. I am told (though

I have never been on the programme myself) that at the lunch The Critics have before recording you can bring your own wine, but that if you do the BBC charges you corkage.

This seems to me to sum up the whole situation if it is true—and even if it isn't.

I had my revenge on the Corporation once, though. Years and years ago, I used to write the script for a weekly programme that was broadcast on the North American Service of BBC radio. There was always a period, when rehearsals had begun (the programme was transmitted in the evening) but before questions of cutting or re-writing had arisen, when I was the only one of the team with nothing to do in the studio. It therefore fell to my lot to go to the canteen and stock up with coffee and biscuits for everybody, a clear breach of the BBC's injunction that crockery was in no circumstances to be taken into the studios.

On this occasion, it had clearly been one of those days. Nobody had had time to eat, and nobody was going to have time to eat. The canteen order, in consequence, resembled nothing so much as the Allies' commissariat requisition on the eve of Waterloo. I staggered out of the canteen bearing a tray piled high with coffee-cups, cheese rolls, salads, ham sandwiches, chocolate-coated digestive biscuits, plaice fried in batter, pots of yoghurt and packets of cigarettes.

I got into the lift and pressed the button with my left ear— the only part of me that was available. Either I pressed the wrong button, or the lift was behaving eccentrically, because when I got out (I could scarcely see over the tray in front of me) and the doors had closed behind me, I realised that I was not only on the wrong floor: I was in a part of the BBC I had never seen before. Lush, wall-to-wall carpet, in a tasteful shade of blue, covered the floor; there was discreet concealed lighting; the doors of the offices I could see were of handsome polished oak.

Had I, I wondered, slipped through some hole in the space-time continuum? Was this Aladdin's cave? *Where the devil was I?* There was only one way to find out, and that was to go and examine the discreet little name-card on the nearest door. With my huge tray of provisions borne on before me, I advanced across the ankle-deep carpet. At exactly the same moment I read the words 'Director-General' on the door and trod heavily on my own instep.

I had to take a very quick decision. Should I try to explain

to the D-G exactly, or even approximately, why I had coated
the door of his office about five inches deep in coffee, rolls and
butter, ham, salad, chocolate-biscuits, cheese, yoghurt and broken
china? Or should I let him try to work it out for himself?

The decision, you understand, had to be taken in the time it
would take a middle-aged man to rise from his desk and walk to
the door of his office, to see if Brutus so unkindly knocked or no.
In the end, I stayed not upon the order of my going. Indeed, I
did not even stay for the lift.

Bordeaux & California — Wine-growing & Wine-drinking in Two Continents

BY ALEC WAUGH

FIRST came to the U.S.A. in the grim days of prohibition, and like other Europeans who hold that a meal without wine is like a day without sunlight, I used sometimes to ask plaintively whether a concession might not eventually be made in favour of light wines and beer. Invariably I received the same reply: 'We have all the beer we need under prohibition, and we have never been a wine-drinking country.' Today, half a lifetime later, that answer with certain reservations still holds good, in spite of the quantity and quality of the wine that is now being produced in California.

Two years ago I made, as the guest of Alexis Lichine, a tour of the great Bordeaux vineyards; in the following fall I visited, as the guest of Martin Ray, the wineries of California—Beaulieu, Inglenook, Almedan, Paul Masson. The difference could not have been greater. In France you can see seven or eight châteaux in a morning; there they stand, dignified and quiet homes with their vineyards round them, and in their outhouses are the rows of fifty-gallon barrels, with their glass stoppers, in which the young wines are waiting to be bottled, while in the cellars underneath, in rack after rack, the wines are ripening in bottle. Not a drop of wine had gone into those casks or barrels that had not come from grapes grown on the estate, so that the labels could bear the imprint *appellation contrôlée*—a device adopted in France in the late 1930s to ensure that the label on a bottle speaks the truth, that the wine comes from one designated area. It is a proof not of quality but of authenticity. A wine that is labelled 'Bourgogne' without the 'appellation contrôlée' guarantee and has possibly been blended with Algerian wine may be richer and pleasanter than an 'appellation contrôlée' burgundy, but in the first case you cannot tell what you are buying: in the second case you can.

In each Bordeaux wine-cellar the ritual was the same. The master—le maître du chais—removed the stopper from one of the casks, inserted a glass funnel, drew up into it a small amount of wine which he would release into a glass and offer it to us to taste. We looked at the '60s and the '61s; they were rough and sour, though 'good upon the nose.' We spat out the sip that we had taken, and the master poured back into the barrel the wine that was left over in the glass. It was a slow ritual. The experts could tell already how the wine that had tasted so sour to me would develop into the rich ambrosia that would eventually stand upon the table.

To a layman like myself it is a miracle that they can. It is the result partly of an acute and highly developed sense of smell, a sensitivity of tongue and palate; partly of the evidence of history, a knowledge based on memory of how a wine should develop given certain conditions of climate, favourable and unfavourable, late frosts and July rains and heavy September sunlight. Yet even so their achievement is remarkable. They are rarely wrong. Their one big mistake in recent years was with the clarets of 1928. Nineteen twenty-eight and 1929 were resplendent summers, and the '29s were ready and delightful by 1936. But the '28s, of which the experts had prophesied far higher qualities, remained obstinately harsh and hard. The experts described them as sulky, and assured their customers that they would mature, as youthful delinquents sometimes do into exemplary citizens. But they never did: or rather only a very few of them did. In 1934 I laid down a case of the '28 Château Latour. I drank the last bottle less than a year ago. It was excellent on the nose, but it had no richness on the tongue.

My unlucky experience with Latour '28 did not, however, tempt me to question Alexis Lichine's estimate of the '60s and '61s. The betting was more than nine to one on his being right.

My trip with Martin Ray in the Napa Valley and south of San Francisco, near Saratoga, was very different. Here there were not small barrels but immense vats that could hold up to 40,000 gallons. Here there was no *appellation contrôlée*. The grapes, the juice of which filled those vats, could within certain limits come from anywhere along the coast. Such limits as there were concerned the kind of grape from which the juice had come. If a bottle is advertised as Pinot Noir or Riesling, then it must contain a certain proportion of wine made from that kind of grape.

In France and Germany, where the climate changes from one year to the next, where certain folds of soil will turn a slope towards the sun and protect the vine shoots against unexpected frost, when protection is thus achieved for one vineyard in one year and in another for the next, one of the chief pleasures for the amateur is the tasting of one year against another, one vineyard against another. But in California the climate is more equable; there is not the same variety of soil; one year is like another and it is good business to aim at a sound standardized product, blending one year's wines with another's. Some wineries do print the date of a wine upon the bottle but others consider that this practice confuses the purchaser; why should he be tempted to differentiate where no actual difference exists? Better that he should concentrate upon the difference between the various varieties of grape, Sémillon and Riesling, Pinot Noir and Gamay.

In California there is no drawing of the wine out of a barrel with a funnel; there is no spitting out of sour fluid. Instead, when the tour of the winery is over, you are taken into a pleasant office and asked which of the House's wines you would prefer to taste; a dry biscuit is brought so that you can clean your palate between sips, and three or four bottles are opened. You taste one against another, and you will have to be very supercilious not to agree that they are sound and balanced; in their own way as good as any except the finest table wines of France and Germany; certainly they are as good as anything that Italy and Spain can offer.

In the Paul Masson winery I was offered a sparkling wine (the law of England prevents my calling it Californian 'Champagne') that is made on the new German system. In the traditional French manner, *la méthode champenoise*, the bottle, during the second fermentation, is tilted downwards and given a slight twist every day so that the sediment collects on the cork. The cork is then removed and a new cork inserted. By the German method the bottle lies on its side while the second fermentation takes place; when this process is completed the bottle is emptied, the wine cleaned and rebottled. It is much quicker and a cheaper process. Said the champagne-master, 'It will take the French a hundred years to realize that this method is as good as theirs.' The wine he showed me was young and gay and fresh. But whether the German method is as good as the French cannot be proved until, in a great year in the champagne area, grapes from the same vineyards are processed by the two different methods, so that a comparison can be made. Great wines, it cannot be repeated too often, are the product of a special year in a special place. Eighty per cent of the non-vintage French champagne is no better than the German Sekt or the best Californian champagne. But the twenty per cent of supreme French champagne is a different thing altogether. It is not recognizable as the same kind of wine.

It is, I repeat, strange to describe as non-wine-drinking a nation that produces so much excellent wine. But the visitor to the United States who soon learns never to be without a hip-flask, so numerous and different are the regulations, state by state and county by county, that restrict his consumption of alcohol, will also learn, if he cares for wine, that it is prudent to arm himself with a corkscrew.

The drinking of wine with meals is so little a general custom that many households do not possess one. I discovered this to my cost in Colorado, when I arrived bearing a bottle of Californian claret as a weekend guest at a cabin in the hills. As there was no corkscrew in the house, we were driven to employ a brace and bit. I held the bottle while my host manipulated the weapon. The result was startling: the cork suddenly disintegrated and the wine exploded like an oil gusher, staining the ceiling red. Martin Ray laughed when I told him that. He was not surprised. 'In some states,' he said, 'that actually presents the Californian wine-merchants with a problem. Some of them don't cork any of the bottles that they send to Illinois. They put caps on them.'

I asked him if that harmed the wine. He shook his head. 'The turnover is very quick. They don't aim at ageing their wines in bottles.'

Martin Ray, a man in his early sixties, is one of the legendary figures in the Californian wine trade. It has long been his contention that given proper care California can produce wines as noble and distinctive as those of France and Germany. Associated in his early years with Paul Masson, he now owns a chain of vineyards high on Mount Eden. He does not blend his wines; his production is small, but every bottle carries a precise definition of its provenance. His big years command an impressively high price.

'There is,' he told me, 'a vast oenological desert between the Appalachians and the Rockies. Almaden, Inglenook, Beaulieu and the rest sell their wines in California, in Louisiana, on the eastern seaboard and in Illinois. Round the edges, in fact.' That desert, as he described it, was colonized when wine was unobtainable. Wine was too bulky to be carried in covered wagons. 'But what about the emigrants themselves?' I asked. 'Didn't they bring their own wine-drinking habits with them?'

Again he shook his head. 'The Italians have always been dependable drinkers of red wine; many five-gallon jars labelled "red paint" crossed the country during Prohibition, but Italians stayed in the cities for the most part; the Scandinavians and the Poles weren't wine-drinkers; the Germans were, but they were happy with beer and schnapps.'

In California it was different, so he explained. There was a long tradition of wine-drinking here. The Spanish mission in San Diego introduced the vine in the third quarter of the eighteenth century. The missions moved up the coast and the Mexican government expanded the industry. Then came the Gold Rush. Naturally it stimulated production: it also brought a new type of emigrant, adventurers rather than settlers, many of whom

---

Gustave Doré drew this jollified and romanticised picture of a *vendange*—probably in the Bordelais—for the *Illustrated London News* in 1858. Parasoled and crinolined, pretty women have come to watch the merry peasants, and the village priest both blesses and imbibes. All a little livelier than life, and yet there is something here still to be recognised at vintage time in the Médoc or the Mâconnais, Champagne or Chateauneuf.

came from wine-drinking countries. Wine had to be found nearer San Francisco, and it was soon discovered that the cool climate of the San Bernadino valley and of the northern counties was admirably suited for the production of table wines, whereas the dry heat of the San Joaquin valley produced grapes with a high sugar content, better suited for dessert wines.

These new emigrants, Martin Ray went on, brought vine cuttings from Europe: for red wines the Cabernet Sauvignon from Bordeaux and the Pinot Noir and Gamay from Burgundy; for white wines the Pinot Chardonnay and Pinot Blanc from Burgundy; the Sylvaner, Traminer and the grey Riesling from Alsace; the Johannisberger Riesling from the Rhine; the Sémillon and Sauvignon Blanc from Bordeaux.

'Our table wines,' Martin Ray concluded, 'are as sound and pleasant as any except the few great wines of France and Germany, but even so we have a hard task ahead to teach the Americans, except those living round the fringe, to take wine with their meals.'

Prohibition did not make their task easier. André Simon, writing in 1938 of the United States, describes them as 'a wine-shy public at all times . . . now hypersensitively suspicious after the dry or semi-dry years of prohibition.' And it must be conceded that Europe has given Americans ample excuse for being wine-shy.

Who would expect Chinese faces in a vineyard? Yet ever since the European vine was taken to California by Spanish missionaries in 1770, 'almost every race which played a part in the building of America,' Schoonmaker and Marvel have written, 'contributed . . . to the creation of California's vineyards and wines.' P. Frenzeny's illustration for *Harper's Weekly* dates from 1878: until about 1890, Californian vineyard labour was almost entirely Chinese. Not all the grapes were trodden: presses were also in use, as can be seen in the larger reproduction on the end-papers.

Much of the literature of wine is superior and complacent, and never has it been more so than during the years immediately following repeal. In 1933 the Wine and Food Society was started in London. Branches were soon opened in the U.S.A. and its members were issued with small ivory cards, showing in which years the various wines were good, poor, or worthless. Englishmen who in the past had been content to enjoy good wine, without worrying about the dates of anything except vintage port, now felt themselves beholden to memorize the classified growths of the Médoc. There was a highly tiresome amount of seemingly knowledgeable talk by men who would have found it hard to tell claret from burgundy unless they had seen the shape of the bottle first.

The nomenclature of wine, most of it based on the French, was freely used. There was talk of *goût de paille*, a musty straw-like flavour, and *goût de pienne à fusil*, a flinty taste to be found in Chablis: there were words like *corsé*, meaning full-blooded; *velouté* (velvety), was a term of recommendation, but *fruité* (fruity) was not. There was talk of the 'robe' of the wine, meaning its colour, and of 'race' meaning its breeding. A *vin de goutte*, which might have been expected to be agreeable, was actually the product of the last pressing and was consequently thin and poor. It is not surprising that many Americans became suspicious of so abstruse and exacting a science. They became shy of serving wine, afraid of doing the wrong thing, preferring to stick to what they knew: cocktails and highballs.

The serving of wine is in fact a simple business, yet it must be recognized that the conditions of modern life do not simplify the drinking of wine during meals. A family sitting down to dinner in their own home can very easily place a bottle of wine upon the table, but when hospitality is involved, lack of servants forces the alternative patterns of the cocktail party and the buffet supper.

Habits in drinking are indeed often determined by the lack or prevalence of servants. When I joined the Savile Club in London, forty years ago, it was the custom after dinner to pass a decanter of vintage port round the table. It was known as Ross's port because Robert Ross's brother Alec had presented a few dozen bottles to the club and the profits on its sale were reinvested in a further supply. Most of us took a glass and sat over it for half an hour or so. Nowadays dining members are encouraged to leave the table early so that the staff can clear up and go home. Last summer I ordered a vintage port and was presented with a glass of brown, muddy wine without smell or flavour. It was explained to me that there was very little demand now for vintage port at any time, and none at all in the summer. That particular wine had been in the decanter for two weeks.

The drinking of wine should be attended with ritual, with the red wine decanted and candlelight shining on polished tables or starched linen, on goblets and on silver. The buffet meal, which owing to a lack of servants is the standard form of entertainment in the U.S.A., is not conducive to wine drinking. The guests are selected with care and they know that they are there for the evening; there is a ninety-minute period for highballs, cocktails or gin-and-tonics and the buffet dinner is as often as not laid in another room. One or two bottles of wine are set on a side table. The glasses beside them are not usually very large. Most of the guests will help themselves to wine; but it is not easy to drink wine when you are balancing a plate on your knees. Both your hands are occupied. You are lucky if you have a table within reach on which to put your glass. You probably put it on the floor, and are afraid that either you or another guest will kick it over. You may put it out of range on a bookcase. That means getting up each time you want a sip. You are not too anxious to move because you are probably sitting beside the woman next to whom you have been planning to sit throughout the evening—its being one of the features of the buffet supper, that during the preliminary ninety minutes of canapés and highballs, you should arrange your campaign so that when you change places after the move to the buffet, you can say to the lady on whom your choice has rested, 'Now this is what I have been looking forward to all the evening.'

The host will make a tour of the room to fill up glasses, but the average dinner guest will probably only take two glasses of wine during his meal. That is barely a fifth of a bottle: for a dinner party seated around a table, a host usually plans on half a bottle a head. At a buffet supper, the dishes are usually cleared within half an hour and one is back to highballs or beer.

Even so the consumption of wines is increasing steadily year by year; and one of the most significant features about this increase is that the rise in demand for table wines is greater than the demand for dessert wines. During 1963, for example, there was an increase of thirteen per cent in consumption of table wines and only three per cent in the consumption of dessert wines. This can only mean that there is a marked new trend towards drinking wine with meals rather than before and after. It may well be that in time the quantity and quality of California's wines will convert the United States to a wine-drinking nation. How this will please the ghost of Thomas Jefferson, who was as incensed by George III's tax on wine as by his tax on tea: 'this aggression on the public taste and comfort,' he called it.

But I do not expect this conversion to take place in my lifetime.

When the dark day comes, as I suppose it must, when doctors limit me to a glass of two of wine at lunch and a resolute eschewing of strong waters, when I sit among my memories in a quiet café-restaurant in the sun, looking out over the blue Mediterranean, and I relive the pleasures of the table, recalling what the Rhine and the Rhône, the Douro and the Gironde have given me, I shall remember how that red sign 'American Bar' has flashed like a harbour light across the lounge of this and the other Ritz, Savoy and Plaza, and I shall think of all the drinks, short and long, cold and highly flavoured, that American ingenuity has blended for my solace. I shall remember mornings in Tucson, reclining on the edge of the swimming pool at the Arizona Inn and sipping a long mint julep; how well the flavour of mint mingled with the heavy Bourbon, and the rough iced glass contrasted with the sunlight. I shall remember cold winter mornings in Chicago, hurrying through the frozen streets that provide such lucrative employment for the specialists in ear, nose and throat afflictions towards the long bar at the United Universities Club, savouring in advance the first sip of an old-fashioned before the ice had robbed the whisky of its warming power; I shall remember in New York on hot summer evenings the peace of the Century Club's balcony and the bitter-sweet coolness of a daiquiri that was served in a small pewter measure beside a frozen glass; and I shall remember the taste of all the extra dry martinis that have preceded lunches, too many to be recounted, and in so many cities and the shock that they have sent to every nerve cell, the first taste not altogether pleasant but with a peace of spirit descending as the level of liquid lowered. Nowhere else in the world does a dry martini taste like that.

Just as the sloping hills between Beaune and Dijon have given to the world its noblest of red wines, and the Douro given its rich port, and the Rhine and Moselle their fragrant white wines, so has America given to the world its scope of recipes and its skill in blending.

And if it is granted to me—as some say it will be—to return briefly from the Elysian Fields to the places that I frequented, and I should find a New York wine list between my hands, I know that I should turn first, not to the vintages of the Napa and Sonoma valleys but to that list of cordials, cocktails, aperitifs and whatnots that Dickens recited like the strophes of a litany, searching for what had survived and what had failed to (what! the Manhattan gone, along with the Orange Blossom and the Bronx?), curious to see what had replaced them, looking for new names, confident that they would be marching proudly under the banner of a long tradition.

To Thea, at the
Year's End — WITH A BOTTLE OF
Gewürztraminer

I have no fancy to define
   Love's fullness by what went before;
I think the day we crossed the line
Was when we drank the sea-cooled wine
   Upon a sun-warmed shore.

The sun in sudden strength that day
   Inflamed the air, but could not reach
The steel-sharp sea of middle May
That brimmed with cold the breathless bay
   Below the sun-drowned beach.

The sun's heat laid its heavy hand
   On unaccustomed skins as we
Went tip-toe down the tilted strand
And set our bottle on the sand
   To cool it in the sea:

And watched as, where the sea-surge spent
  The last of its quiescent strength,
Stone-cold and circumambient,
The intermittent water went
  Along its polished length.

The bottle took the water's cold
  But did not let its wetness pass;
Glinting and green the water rolled
Against the wine's unmoving gold
  Behind its walls of glass.

We cooled it to our just conceit
  And drank. The cold aroma came
Almost intolerably sweet
To palates which the salt and heat
  Had flayed as with a flame.

We swam and sunned as well as drank,
  And found all heaven in a word;
But, dearest Thea, to be frank,
I think we had the wine to thank
  For most of what occurred.

And now the winter is to waste,
  I bring a bottle like the first;
And this in turn can be replaced,
As long as we have tongues to taste,
  And God shall give us thirst,

Lest with the year our love decline,
  Or like the summer lose its fire,
Before the sun resurgent shine
To warm the sea that cooled the wine
  That kindled our desire.

P. M. HUBBARD

'An Universal Hospitality' — the *Old Dominion*'s Open Door

BY JOAN PARRY DUTTON

ENEROUS housekeeping and good entertainment had been a characteristic of English country gentlemen for generations before Charles II elevated the colony of Virginia to the status of a Dominion—the 'Old Dominion'—by quartering its arms upon his own. So it was natural that the colonists, who set out to make Virginia another corner of the Mother Country, followed the old familiar pattern, and even in quite early days of settlement hospitality and good food and drink were as much a part of Virginian life as were its virgin forests, and its maze of waterways. In the 1620s even, an official report *A Briefe Declaration of Virginia* noted that the quantity of provisions of all kinds was so great that every man gave free entertainment to his friends and to strangers. The homeland's view of the open door was broadened to include the humblest passer-by—though they were served elsewhere than in the front of the manor house.

By the end of the seventeenth century a tradition of hospitality was established. Wrote a Virginia planter-historian, Robert Beverly, Gent.:

Here is the most Good-nature, and Hospitality practis'd in the World, both towards friends and strangers. . . . The Inhabitants are very courteous to Travellers, who need no other Recommendation but the being human Creatures. A Stranger has no more to do, but to inquire upon the Road, where any Gentleman, or good Housekeeper lives, and there he may depend upon being received with Hospitality.

It was the same in good tobacco years or bad. There was plenty of food for all, and plenty of servants—first the indentured servant and then the Negro—to prepare and serve groaning boards of food and drink. And the isolation and loneliness of plantation life made a chance visitor more than welcome, and when coming from afar every traveller was a walking or horseback newspaper.

With the growing prosperity of the eighteenth century, the Old Dominion's golden age, hospitality really warmed up. In the July 1746 issue of *The London Magazine* an observing traveller just back from Virginia reported:

All over the Colony, an universal Hospitality reigns; full tables and open doors, the kind salute, the generous detention, speak somewhat like the old roast-beef ages of our forefathers, and would almost persuade one to think their shades were wafted into these regions, to enjoy with greater extent the reward of their virtues.

And our traveller goes on:

What is said here is most strictly true, for their manner of living is quite generous and open: strangers are sought after with greediness, as they pass through the country, to be invited. Their breakfast tables have generally the cold remains of the former day, hash'd or fricasseed; coffee, tea, chocolate, venison-pasty, punch, and beer, or cyder, upon one board; their dinner, good beef, veal, mutton, venison, turkies and geese, wild and tame, fowls, boil'd and roasted; and perhaps somewhat more, as pies, puddings, etc., for dessert: suppers the same, with some small addition, and a good hearty cup to precede a bed of down: and this is the constant life they lead, and to this fare every comer is welcome.

The fare, indeed, betokened a plenty beyond any other people of that day. Grown rich as tobacco-planters, the colonists enjoyed every table luxury known to England plus a goodly array that were the New World's own, with Virginia's the cream.

As then, the Old Dominion was confined mostly to what is called The Tidewater, a triangle of land and waterways less than a quarter the size of England, flat, marshy low-land country fronting in part on the ocean and mainly on Chesapeake Bay, an inland sea.

Four great rivers, the James, the York, the Rappahannock and the Potomac, each rising and falling with the tides, together with an endless tangle of outlets, bays and tributary streams comparable in size to the Thames, make the Tidewater a maze of land and water, the virgin soil of which was a rock-free sandy loam in which anything would grow, sped on by a mild climate and a benign rainfall. The forests and the marshes teemed with game and wild fowl. Land was so abundant and springs so plentiful that horses, hogs and cattle were released to roam and multiply at will. Wild berries, grapes and nuts were everywhere, and then there were the Red Indian's contributions to a goodly life: Indian corn or maize, beans, peas, yams and other vegetables of varieties new to Europe, together with such refinements to civilized living as planked shad and roe.

The runs of shad and sturgeon in spring were fabulous, the fish filling the streams literally by the millions. So with many other kinds of fish and shell fish—oysters larger than the best of Colchester's. There were places when the tide was out where oysters could be scraped up by bucketfuls.

It was a silk-and-satin society, swords with hilts of gold, silver shoe-buckles, farthingales and powdered wigs; of coaches and Negro slaves, the household servants often being dressed in livery. Most of the larger plantations—from 5,000 to 100,000 acres was rated large—had their plantation-house fronting the river highway. Ships from abroad could unload goods at the planter's own doorside wharves, and take on board hogsheads of tobacco that paid the bills and usually left a profit. Wealthy planters and their wives occasionally spent the winter season in London; sons often attended English schools.

Williamsburg, named after William III, was the colonial capital: a little city that resembled a good country town in England with its mile-long Duke of Gloucester Street, its College of William and Mary, its Capitol and Court House and Government House. One royal governor had completed the House in such determined extravagance, backed by heavy levies, that irate taxpayers dubbed it The Governor's Palace. Above all floated the Grand Union flag of Queen Anne's reign.

Williamsburg was the centre of official hospitality. In character a country town most of the year, it assumed the air of a metropolis during 'Publick Times'—special celebrations, royal birthdays, above all when the Assembly and the Courts met twice a year, in spring and fall. At such times the burden of hospitality drained every official's purse, not least the governor's. Governor Gooch, writing to his brother (later a Bishop of Norwich), frequently voiced his apprehension that his present high rate of living would prevent his retiring to a fair retreat in old age, and that he would have to walk on foot after riding so long in his coach and six.

The victory of Culloden provided one such celebration. When the news reached Virginia on 18 July, 1746:

. . . In the Evening a very numerous Company of Gentlemen and Ladies appear'd at the Capitol, where a Ball was open'd, and after dancing some Time, withdrew to Supper, there being a very handsome Collation spread on three Tables, in three different Rooms, consisting of near 100 Dishes, after the most delicate Taste. There was also provided a great Variety of the choicest and best Liquors, in which the Healths of the King, the Prince and Princess of Wales, the Duke, and the rest of the Royal Family, the Governor, Success to his Majesty's Arms, Prosperity to this Colony, and many other loyal Healths were cheerfully drank, and a Round of Cannon, which were remov'd to the Capitol for this Purpose, was discharg'd at each Health, to the Number of 18 or 20 Rounds, which lasted 'til near 2 o'Clock. The whole Affair was conducted with great Decency and good Order, and an unaffected Chearfullness appeared in the Countenances of the Company. All the Houses in the City were illuminated, and a very large Bon-fire was made in the Market-Place, 3 Hogsheads of Punch given to the Populace; and the whole concluded with the greatest Demonstrations of Joy and Loyalty.

As well it might be.

What went on in Williamsburg went on, in varying degrees, throughout the Tidewater. Entertainment was constant and wholesale, and there was an incredible amount of drinking, far more than in England, itself far from arid. For one thing, there was greater prosperity. As one English traveller put it: 'I am well convinced that I could have lived much better and made more money, as a Farmer in this country, with five hundred pound, than I can in England, with two thousand.' Also, in the low-lying Tidewater, alcoholic liquor was regarded as a preventative against the prevalent fever and flux. The early-rising planter

A Design to represent the beginning and completion of an American SETTLEMENT or FARM.

Painted by Paul Sandby, from a Design made by h

London, Printed for John Bowles at N.º 13, in Cornhill, Robert Sayer at N.º 53, in Fleet Street, Tho. Jeff.

Dessein qui represente la manière d'etablir et de parachever une Habitation ou FERME AMERICAINE.

Governor Pownal. Engraved by James Peake.

going his rounds on horseback in the cool of summer mornings invariably fortified himself with a starter, and there were desperate longings for a quencher in the long sweltering afternoons.

Yet the Virginia planter ordinarily conducted himself with the same 'great Decency and good Order' as did the company at the celebration ball. A gentleman was expected to carry his liquor as a gentleman should. Rarely was he seen half-seas over, and there is no record of a situation such as John Evelyn twice described, when servants were instructed to ply guests until they were under the table.

Tidewater Virginia, smaller than England and less populated, offered no anonymity. Unlike London, Williamsburg was only a small town. No gentleman could be lost in the crowd. Everybody knew him, from the governor down to the humblest servant or slave. Besides, he had to set an example. He was a trader, a man of business, as well as a countryman and, like the squire, he was a public servant, taking his place in the Assembly or on the Council as squires took theirs on the Bench or in the House of Commons. With tobacco-growing needing many hands he had a large labour force which was mostly black—in 1740 black faces outnumbered white.

One of the planter's big problems was keeping the Negro servants sober. A royal governor once made a bargain with his, that if they would forbear to drink upon the Queen's Birthday, when he was officially entertaining, they might be drunk at will on the morrow. William Byrd II, master of the great Westover plantation, spanked his maids when he caught them stealing his rum and filling up the bottle with water. He deplored the effect of cheap rum on Negroes, though he had inherited a fortune from his trader-father who imported incredible quantities of rum from the West Indies.

Yet William Byrd II, one of the most cultured and distinguished men of his day, would have regarded prohibition as uncivilized. Educated in England, he was a member of the Middle Temple and the Royal Society, a lifetime friend of Sir Robert Southwell and of Charles Boyle, Earl of Orrery. He was a member of the Virginia Council, finally its President, and throughout many years of his life kept a diary as Samuel Pepys had done, in shorthand.

Few gentlemen drank deeper than Byrd, but he summed up his attitude on the subject when he jotted down one day's happening: 'the parson and I returned to our quarters in good time and good order, but my man Tom broke the rules of hospitality by getting extremely drunk in a civil house.' And he noted that he was very much surprised when he discovered a lady of some note, and of unhappy marriage, drinking too much, even though her relatives, 'disguise it under the name of consolation.'

Toasting could be something of a test, for somebody was always proposing a bottoms-up toast to somebody else. How deeply the habit had taken hold is illustrated by the annals of the Knights of the Golden Horse Shoe. That title was conferred by a royal governor upon ten gentlemen who accompanied him, along with two companies of Rangers and four Indian guides, on an expedition of discovery into the western mountains. All the horses had to be specially shod for the journey over rough trails, because in the stoneless Tidewater horses were seldom shod. Later, the governor presented each gentleman with a golden horseshoe in memory of the trip.

The records set forth that other necessities of the rough westward journey through Indian country included several casks of Virginia wine, red and white, Irish whiskey, brandy, shrub, two kinds of rum, champagne, Canary, cherry punch, and cider, etc.

When the expedition gained 'the very top of the Appalachians,' the highest mountain was named Mount George for the King and, 'We drank to the King's health and all the royal family's.' Next day they crossed the broad Shenandoah River, no mean feat, and the governor claimed all the land beyond in the King's name. This was the journey's climax and was appropriately celebrated.

'We had a good dinner,' wrote the chronicler, 'and after we got the men together, and loaded all their arms, we drank the King's health in champagne, and fired a volley; the Princess's health in burgundy, and fired a volley; and all the rest of the royal family's in claret and fired a volley. We drank the Governor's health and fired another volley.'

I know of no other instance where English explorers in a hostile wilderness have staged so brave a show for King, country and Bacchus.

The Tidewater's mansions and fine cellars were in remote lonely forests, reached only by boat or rough dirt-track roads through the long woods, like the fairy castles of childhood tales. Plantation houses were smaller than English country houses, but they were lived in from top to bottom by family and friends, there being at least one bed in every room except the kitchen. The

servants lived separately in their own quarters grouped around the big house.

Visiting was a favourite pastime. By the middle of the eighteenth century, some three hundred Tidewater families, all closely related by intermarriage, made up the ruling top-planter class. With almost everybody who was anybody on kissin'-cousin terms, visiting was entirely informal. Travel being uncertain and swift communication lacking, the frequent and unexpected arrival of guests was commonplace. People would drive or ride up, send the horses to the stable, and walk into the house as welcome guests; stay a week, move on from one plantation to another, and be away from home by the month.

A Frenchman who spent one Christmas under the roof of a great plantation house recounts how one day his host and other guests decided, on the spur of the moment, to see some of the plantation's holdings, and then go on to the home of a neighbouring planter:

. . . so we rode twenty strong to Colonel Fichous' but he has such a large establishment that he did not mind. We were all of us provided with beds, one for two men. He treated us royally, there was good wine & all kinds of beverages, so there was a great deal of carousing. He had sent for three fiddlers, a jester, a tight-rope dancer, an acrobat who tumbled around, & they gave us

---

Building scenes such as this must have been a pretty common sight in eighteenth–century Colonial Virginia. Thomas Maitland Cleland, designer, typographer and painter who died at the age of eighty-four in November 1964, was never happier than when drawing such scenes. He was a very outspoken critic of most modern art and especially architecture, which he dismissed as 'quackery'. The drawing is continued from page 37.

all the entertainment one could wish for. It was very cold, yet no one ever thinks of going near the fire, for they never put less than a cartload of wood in the fireplace & the whole room is kept warm. . . . The next day, after they had caroused until after noon, we decided to cross the river. The Colonel had a quantity of wine & one of his punch-bowls brought to the shore; he lent us his boat.

There were, of course, the usual family gatherings; affairs that might last several days, with balls, cockfights, horse races and a back-room card game that ran continuously. Dinner, at such family assemblies, would be around four o'clock. 'For Drink there were several sorts of wine, good lemon punch, toddy, cyder, porter, etc.' Dancing was, 'first minuets one round, second giggs, third reels, and last of all country dances, tho they struck several marches occasionally. The music a French Horn and 2 violins. Ladies dressed gay and splendid, and when dancing, their silks and brocades rustled and trailed behind them.'

Those who travelled many miles for weddings and funerals were extraordinarily well provided for. At one funeral in 1667, twenty-five gallons of beer, twenty-two gallons of cider, five of brandy, and twelve pounds of sugar went into the expense account.

The listings of mixed drinks show there was no etiquette that laid down rules for certain wines being served with certain foods. As in England, the Virginians' taste was for foreign wines and, surprisingly, inns and taverns were often as well stocked with these as were plantation cellars. In addition, casks of Virginia beer, cider and perry, mead, peach brandy, cordial and other home-distilled spirits were as commonplace as corn-bread.

Price is some indication of taste—it was fixed by law at inns and taverns. Virginia ale was twopence per quart, Madeira upwards of two shillings, and nearly twice as much for claret.

Madeira was imported in return for staves for barrel-making, wheat and other Virginian products. On occasion a group of planters would charter a ship, load it with wheat, corn and planking and despatch it to Madeira in exchange for a cargo of wine.

Madeira was not a fortified wine in those days, and would have contained about 12/15% alcohol (as against today's 18%). If the wine was spoiled by being cloudy due to cold, heat would revive it, as William Byrd II knew very well. It is, he said, 'unlike any other wine if spoil'd, which happens mostly because of coldness, one may place it in the strongest and warmest heat of sun, where it regains its quality in a very few days and is completely restored as before.' He also observed that the storing of sound Madeira in a warm place would be very good for the wine, and perhaps he had no need to know that no wine lasts longer than a Madeira: 'a good Madeira never reaches senility.'

Thomas Jefferson was the acknowledged connoisseur of food and wine, although Patrick Henry denounced him in a political speech as a man who had 'abjured his native victuals' and was unfaithful to good, old-fashioned roast beef. This was after Jefferson's five years in France as Minister to the Court of Louis XVI.

For Jefferson, who loved extravagant and subtle dishes, wine was 'a necessity of life.' Having no good word for whisky, he declared as any Frenchman might that, 'No nation is drunk where wine is cheap.' He also had a strong liking for cider and the best West Indian rum. His cellar was full, and contained a quantity of twelve-year-old Antigua rum when the British took Richmond and drank his cellar dry. Isaac, one of Jefferson's slaves, later recalled that, 'Isaac never heard of his being disguised in drink.'

Claret was undoubtedly George Washington's preference. When the Marquis de Chastellux gave him a cask, he said: 'You can relieve me by promising to partake very often of that hilarity which a Glass of good Claret seldom fails to produce.'

As the Golden Age drew towards its close, with Tidewater soil depleted by over-intensive tobacco-growing, and with many eyes already turning westward, many of the greater planters found the old-style hospitality a burden they could no longer support. And, by this time, rivers were no longer the main highways. Travel by land was easier. Roads, even if still dirt tracks, made sweeping roundabout curves to cross creeks at shallow fords or by raft-like ferries poled back and forth between the banks. Virginians usually drove six horses, travelling eight to nine miles an hour, frequently going sixty miles for dinner.

George Washington, who loved the simple domestic life of a private gentleman at Mount Vernon, ruefully concluded, after he became President, that Mount Vernon had become more like 'a well-resorted inn.' It was the same with Thomas Jefferson who, tiring of seating fifty unexpected guests to dinner, was well-nigh eaten out of house and home. He built himself another house a hundred miles or so from Monticello, where he retired from the burdens of hospitality three or four times a year.

So with Fitzhugh of Chatham. His great house being close by the much-travelled main road running south to north, and himself being connected with many of the wealthiest families, some one or other of them, travelling in their coaches, was always coming to visit him. It seemed as though the stream to and from his ever-open door would never cease. Finally, realizing hospitality was breaking his fortune he, too, built another house in a more remote part of the country where he could enjoy economic retirement. Many a man would have remembered as did Fitzhugh's old friend George Washington: 'I have put my legs oftener under your mahogany at Chatham than anywhere else in the world, and have enjoyed your good dinners, good wine and good company more than any other.' One could hardly wish for warmer words from an old friend, but then, as one traveller wrote of the Virginians of the eighteenth century in his *Retrospections of America*: 'their conviviality was like their own summers, as radiant as it was warm.'

The Raleigh Tavern, Williamsburg

My Goodness . . .

BY GERARD FAY

'Ireland sober is Ireland free'
But Guinness still is good for me.

HIS slogan is all my own work, and I am willing
to sell it to Arthur Guinness Son & Co., Ltd.,
modestly conceding that it is not quite as snappy
as some of their own. But it has a slight sub-
liminal quality designed to convey an idea about Guinness
in the history of Ireland. The first line is a famous
aphorism developed and spread after the amazing success of
Father Mathew's great temperance mission of the mid-nineteenth
century. His work imposed voluntarily a Great Thirst on hundreds
of thousands of Irishmen during and after the Great Hunger, and
its effects remain today. There are still, proportionately, more
total abstainers in Ireland than in most European countries.

The second line is based on one of the Company's most
successful advertising catch-phrases. Taken together, they are to
suggest that what is good for Guinness is good for Ireland—an
idea that was current long before General Motors was heard of
—and that making fortunes out of brewing does not exclude
being fanatically interested in the welfare of a nation. Only the

bluest of bluenoses would suggest that Guinness have done more harm than good or deny that they had consistently influenced the country's economy.

Wherever zymurgy is practised there will be Irish names not only among the consumers but among the producers, too. Hennessys rub shoulders with Martells and Courvoisiers, a Lynch can be neighbour to a Rothschild, and there is the unsolved mystery of whether Haut Brion does not really stem from O'Brien, as many other good things do.

Holding their own with Basses, Ratcliffes, Grettons, Trumans, Hanburys and Buxtons, the greatest of the Irish zymurgists are undoubtedly the Guinnesses. No doubt there were those who called the first John Jameson, Jack, but he never seems to emerge as a figure, whereas the Guinnesses constitute a whole procession that has been going on for two centuries of outstanding men and—although this had nothing to do with the family business —of spirited and beautiful women.

To anybody who is being brought up in Dublin it is soon clear that the word Guinness has a particular connotation. In its first use it does not, as in England, mean stout: on the contrary, in Dublin 'stout' means Guinness and it is a hard thing for the Irishman coming to London or Liverpool or Manchester to get used to the idea that there are other brewers who claim to produce 'stout', or that there are even such variations as oatmeal stout or milk stout. No, the special meaning of Guinness in Dublin is first the brewery, a really enormous one, which in Irish eyes makes Dublin the Detroit of the stout industry. Secondly, it means the family that left its mark in the most obvious ways by providing work in a largely non-industrial country at higher than average pay. 'You cannot,' said Edward Cecil Guinness, later the first Lord Iveagh, 'expect to make money out of people unless you are prepared to let them make money out of you.' In less obvious ways the family left its mark by always keeping a firm hand on the Irish banking system, not only through the revered firm of Guinness & Mahon, but through the Bank of Ireland itself, which is not one of your poor wishy-washy nationalised bodies like the Bank of England—it sometimes pays as high as 20% dividend on its shares.

As surely as it stood for commercial success, probity and millionaire richness, the name Guinness also stood for a world of fashion and of a sweet life far away from the industrial processes and economic experiments of St James's Gate in the old part of Dublin dominated by the Liffey and by the two Cathedrals, one rebuilt by a Guinness, which still stand for a reminder that at one time all power in Ireland was in the hands of those who preferred an 'alien' form of Christianity.

At one extreme Guinness stood for hard work and high thinking (but without any Quakerish opposition to the fine arts) and at

SAINT JAMES'S GATE

the other it stood for the world of race-horses and elegant women, hunting, fishing, shooting, living in castles, rubbing shoulders with kings and princes and Mitfords and Kindersleys and More O'Ferralls. One Guinness entry in Debrett firmly refers the inquirer to the chapter called 'Royal Family'. This is because a daughter (living) of the second Earl married Friedrich Georg Wilhelm Christoph von Preussen.

No doubts, then about the family: no doubts about the product either. 'The comeliest of black malts is, of course, that noble liquor called of Guinness. Here at least I think England cannot match Ireland, for our stouts are, as a rule, too sweet and

"clammy"'. This was George Saintsbury's only comment on stout
—but 'noble liquor' is not to be sneezed at from so critical a
writer. Without any of the literary trimmings, I used to hear
much the same from my grandmother, a robust Gaelic speaker
from County Galway, who, like so many of her countrywomen,
arrived in this country ignorant of English but aware of the
virtues of Guinness. She used to drink it, preferably, in the
kitchen of her favourite public house, the Princess Royal, which
I do not doubt got its title from that German part of the Royal
Family with which the Guinnesses are connected. This was of
no interest to my grandmother, to whom Guinness was a form of
nutrition, not a great family. If something temporarily prevented
her attendance at the Princess Royal she used to send me out for
some stout in a white jug which held about a quart and cost a
small handful of pennies. She let me taste it once—and once
was enough. I can swear that not being a woman of any literary
enthusiasm, she had never read or heard Charles Stuart Calverley's
lines:

> 'O Beer! O Hodgson, Guinness, Allsopp, Bass
> Names that should be on every infant's tongue'.

I thought my occasional sip horrid, but it was nectar to her
and when she ever thought of calling it anything but just 'stout'
she pronounced the word 'Guinness' with reverence.

Later on I used to hear the name Guinness from a great-aunt
who lived in a most unfashionable part of Dublin near St Patrick's
Cathedral. She was what I suppose could be called a slum-
landlord but hardly a combatant in the class-war since she gave
away to her tenants much more than she ever drew in rent. In
her part of the Liberties of Dublin there were many Guinness
Trust dwellings, cold-looking, miserable-seeming places by modern
standards, but like Peabody or Sutton dwellings (and for that
matter some Guinness buildings) in London they were the
exemplary up-to-date expression of how the Victorian do-gooder
thought he could do best in housing the working class. To my
great aunt Lizzie they were something of a danger or threat
to the faithful. The Guinness family was much struck by
revelations about slums and city landlordism which were made
with greater frequency when the country was launched into a
new period of prosperity after the great famine. Much of the
building done for the labouring classes in Dublin was indistinguish-

able from what was going up in Lancashire or the Black Country at the same time. These were, in the 'sixties and 'seventies, believed to be an improvement for families that had been living in sixteenth-century hovels near the Guinness-restored St Patrick's Cathedral, or in the former mansions of the gentry who had been making a slow departure (which later became a rout) from Dublin, leaving behind them solid tall houses which became tenements and remained a characteristic Dublin eyesore for far too many decades. Guinness policy was first to build sturdy houses for its own employees and then extend the good work to the much larger number of the poor who huddled around the Cathedrals and were beginning to throw outposts north of the river.

One of the marginal benefactions to be found among the bright red Guinness Trust dwellings was known as 'the bayno'—presumably 'beano' translated—which consisted of a cup of cocoa, a bun and some organised games. I went to it once with some local gangsters aged about eight to whom I had formed a temporary attachment. My great-aunt was shocked and ashamed and told me never to do it again.

Still, she was as ready to praise Guinness's good works as she was to blame the stout and porter which brought her tenants to the poverty which made the good works necessary. She was wideminded enough to realise that poverty and squalor were more immediate and therefore to be fought with more vigour than heresy and impiety as supported by the Church of Ireland. She was realist enough also to admit that although the only good thing that came from the brewery was the smell, brewery-workers, of whatever faith, were properly fed and dressed and housed which was more than she could say about most of her neighbours. The smell, by the way, was one of the minor pleasures of Dublin childhood on malting days—as the smell of bulk tobacco must be in Bristol or Nottingham or Clerkenwell.

Long before the war an advertising copywriter thinking on the lines of Pink Pills for Pale People started work on a slogan which was to begin 'Black Beer for . . .' Even in those less sensitive days he realised that the line had better not be followed—yet he had a prophetic soul, for one of the big Guinness enterprises of today is a brewery in Nigeria selling black beer mainly to black people. It is always as well to remember that stout or porter are black beers of a particular strength and flavour and not some magically different brew.

FOUNDER AND FIRST ADVERTISEMENT

A FINE POSTER BY TOM ECKERSLEY

As a Dublin boy I naturally came to regard Guinness and stout as synonyms, and beer as something drunk by eccentrics or Englishmen—who were often the same people. The Dubliners who took to ale showed what seemed a clear contempt for the stuff by sprinkling fruit cordial into it—a row of cordial-shakers stood on every bar and the choice included raspberry. That is a wheel that has come full circle, for Guinness now own a company that brews lager beer and people actually drink it with lime-juice added. (I once saw and overheard a party of English in a café in France trying to order lager and lime; not only was it beyond the waiter's comprehension that anybody should want to put anything in beer—even English beer—but as the man had taken the wrong 'lime' from the dictionary and was asking for *jus de chaux*, the waiter also feared that his customer was up to some mass-poisoning plot.)

Beer it is, then, but black—'stout' because it is strong, 'porter' because London porters were fond of a black beer which was cheaper than stout. As in other breweries, a mash is made of malt and barley with hot water to turn the starches into sugar. The water for Guinness comes from springs in the next county of Kildare and the water is one of the ingredients of the special taste. The mash becomes wort, to be boiled with hops as a pre-servative and a flavouring. Then come the yeast and the fermentation to bring in the alcohol and the carbon-dioxide which provide the kick in the drink and the froth on the top of it. Before being bottled or put into casks the beer has to be stabilised for flavour, which is done by blending different brews.

As Guinness is beer, it is subject to all the complications of cellarage and of being properly kept—though the introduction of metal casks has done away with a lot of this.

There were once three Mooneys near each other in London—Holborn, Fleet Street and, to fortify the walker's spirits between the two, Fetter Lane. Before the coming of Formica the Fleet Street one was distinguished by being more like a genuine Dublin pub than anything left in the City of Dublin itself—neither Fetter Lane nor Holborn was of the right shape. The argument often raged about which of the three produced the best pint of Guinness, and the verdict usually went to Fetter Lane because of some virtue in the cellarage. To a coarse palate the Fetter Lane pint seemed as smooth as any drawn in any Dublin pub chosen by serious-minded drinkers as a 'good house for a pint.' Visiting

Dubliners denied this and would have none of the English blarney about Park Royal brewery being the equal of St James's Gate. But the argument is seldom heard now—the Holborn Mooney's closed when a lease expired: the others both use metal containers and both continue to sell their large and increasing quota.

Perhaps I have put too much stress on the family, on paternalism, tradition and history. If this gives the impression that Guinness is an old-fashioned firm I could hardly be more misleading.

To use a financial jargon word Guinness has gone a long way in diversification—almost entirely in trades logically connected with its own. In Ireland there is a link with Ind Coope to produce ales and the same subsidiary, Irish Ale Breweries, in its turn, is linked through the Irish Cider and Perry Co. with Showerings of Shepton Mallet hence with Babycham and Bulmers' Ciders. The same chain reaction gives Guinness an interest in some wholesale wine and spirit firms controlled by Grants of St James's.

In partnership with a Dutch firm, Guinness run Crookes Laboratories, working primarily on fermentation and the behaviour of yeast and barley. A Dublin subsidiary, Industrial Mouldings (Ireland) Ltd. produces beer crates and milk crates, and the Camac Cask Company produces metal containers for home use and for export. Hop farms, maltings and transport, are other subsidiaries hived off from the master company but a new departure is Guinness (Nigeria) Ltd. which brews in Ikeja and sells all over the country.

A subsidiary not in any way concerned with brewing is the Nuttall Group through which Guinness own Mintoes, Callard and Bowser's butterscotch and 180 confectioners, tobacconists and newsagents in Great Britain. And, of course, there is the *Guinness Book of Records*, which has grown into a big business controlled by its own company.

What is to be seen by a peep into the great central hall of the head office at St James's Gate might hint at an old-fashioned firm—brass plates, massive counters and panelling are everywhere in a gigantic version of a Victorian counting-house. But it does not take long to find out—as the diversification shows—that on its rock-hard foundations of eighteenth-and nineteenth-century industrial and commercial methods Guinness has built a 100% modern business empire. This has been done without any of the harshness or hardness that sometimes go with the making of very big business. Guinness has almost from the beginning not only treated its employees very well but taken them into the company's confidence and encouraged them to make careers rather than just doing jobs.

It must have been a shock to some of the older hands when in 1929 Guinness went in for advertising on a large scale and produced posters and slogans which for subtlety and originality, design and impact were revolutionary and have remained far ahead in the field of imaginative hard-selling copy. They are cleverly translated into the languages of every country where Guinness is sold, including Irish.

Much of this work, and of the company's publicity, is done with an apparent artlessness that I have always suspected conceals a number of needle-sharp master minds. I might give an example of how Guinness, without beating any drums about it, quietly suggests that it is not as other companies are. Look in the London telephone directory—how many other gigantic companies will give you separate telephone numbers where the chief executives can be reached 'after office hours'?

The Guinness annual general meetings are held in London, not Dublin, and this year (1965) the chairman's report was one to make the shareholders echo the slogan 'Guinness is good for you'. As a good proportion of them are in the licensed trade in Ireland (where tied houses are very rare indeed) the chairman has to address himself—in print at any rate—to as knowledgeable a lot of shareholders as exist in any industry. How fortunate for him to be able to record sales of Guinness the highest in the company's history; profits up 16% on the previous year and also the highest ever recorded; dividend 21% compared with 19.2%; overseas sales still expanding in spite of the third best foreign market having been lost (Ghana no longer imports Guinness); the Harp Lager consortium doing better than expected. There was even a famous legal victory to be recorded, described thus by Lord Elveden: 'At the end of a specially successful trading year, when the quality of Guinness has been kept uniformly higher than ever before, let us not forget to salute the famous Guinness head, whose essential role as part of what we regard as the best drink in the world has this year been preserved, we hope for ever, in the Courts.'

If at first sight this seems to refer to something else I might put in the reminder that in a weights and measures prosecution it was finally held that the froth is part of the drink and that a pint includes the white collar, a situation that could be changed fairly quickly, allowing for the law's delays, if our reformed weights and measures system were ever to make the oversize glass a legal reality: at present its value is hygienic and aesthetic; it could revolutionise the draught-beer trade by establishing full measure and no spillage.

Whether you look at it as just a brewery or as part of Ireland's economic life, as a paternalistic family business or as a go-ahead public company (which it became in 1886) it is hard not to notice Arthur Guinness Son & Co. Ltd. Old establishments, family businesses, deep-rooted traditions are common to all sides of brewing, distilling and wine-making. There are good, logical reasons for this. They derive from the peculiar nature of zymurgy, and they can all be seen working yeastily on Guinness breweries in Dublin, London or Ikeja.

Days with Brendan Behan — Drawing and Drinking in Dublin and New York

A PORTFOLIO BY PAUL HOGARTH

RENDAN BEHAN once said that he didn't give a damn whether an artist was abstract or representational, just so long as he wasn't teetotal. Happily, I qualified as an imbibing realist for our books on Ireland and New York,* working on the one in his company, and on the other in his wake—if wake is not too ambiguous a word in the context.

I remember sailing with him on a day trip from Galway to the Isle of Inishore in the Aran Islands. We sailed one sunny morning and the steamer was crowded with fishermen returning

*Brendan Behan's Island, 1962; and Brendan Behan's New York, 1964.

home. The day started with a monologue on Joyce and Shaw, laced with oaths, delivered by Brendan to a baffled group of teetotal English tourists. We adjourned to the womb-like bar lounge down in the inside of the ship. In the smoke, a dark-eyed girl was lugubriously intoning the more sentimental songs of the Irish. Brendan listened for a minute or two and then became restless. He could stand it no longer and burst out into a rousing I.R.A. song about sudden death in Crossley tenders outside the old town of Macoom. The fishermen were silent, but Brendan sang on, stopping only to make sure that everyone had a big glass of stout in their fists. The company began to respond; voices joined Brendan's in spirited renderings of rebel song. The girl had long been silenced. Stout flowed like water. Two hours and two hundred songs later, the boat steamed into Kilronan harbour with a merry company of two hundred singing fishermen. Still singing, we left the ship led by Brendan up the quayside heading for the nearest and only bar, to have one for the road.

It was in just such frolicking, always led by Behan, that I drew most of the bar interiors and characters for *Brendan*

Behan's Island. It was different in New York, for he had gone on ahead of me—and yet not so different, for his memory was so fresh and so fragrant in the bars and saloons of downtown New York that it was almost as if one could still hear the echoes of the roistering.

1 There is McSorley's, an old Irish alehouse on East Seventh Street, to begin with. I knew the place from the drawings and paintings of John Sloan long before I visited America. It was a favourite haunt of the Ashcan painters in the years before the First World War. It doesn't seem to have changed much since then. Most London pubs with the same sort of associations have been demolished or 'remodelled' years ago. On the floor caked sawdust. On the walls memorabilia of countless bygone convivialities. No women allowed. Only ale from the wood is sold—dark or light—twenty cents for one or thirty for two. The barman watches your speed and says, why not have the double, save yourself a dime? In the parlour behind you can have cheeses of every kind, raw onion rings with good fresh bread served with your ale on scrubbed wooden-topped iron tables.

A gallery of priest-like elders line the wall opposite the great mahogany bar with its ornate spittoons and worn brass footrail. Their company cannot be bought lightly. They are the guardians of McSorley's, and keep the place inviolate for the affairs of men, although the joint is owned by a woman.

2 Then there is the Silver Rail on the corner of West 23rd Street and 7th Avenue. A bar much used by Dylan Thomas and Brendan Behan. 'Whatever happened to those two fat guys? They wuz good company!' At night the Silver Rail radiates an inviting brilliance reminiscent of Van Gogh's *Night Café at Arles*. The company here is somewhat predatory-looking, dividing its time between the Horn and Hardart automat next door, the sidewalk and the bar itself. Sometimes the company is leavened by a small circle of fragile, bird-like actresses who talk about the old days when 23rd Street was the centre of the theatre district and everyone who was anyone dined at Cavanagh's.

3 Brendan was a little afraid of the Silver Rail ('Jasus, it's like lookin' in on the ould newsreels'). He preferred the more genial Oasis, a bistro-type bar two or three doors down, towards the Hotel Chelsea. The chromium-plated Oasis has little style and no atmosphere to speak of but at that time it had Willy Garfinkle, a golden-hearted proprietor, laying down the law. His good woman Jeannie worked with him, looking after the kitchen. They were good friends to Brendan and ran an honest-to-goodness place where you ate a good steak, took your liquor straight, created good talk and no fancy business.

WILLY GARFINKLE of the OASIS

4 Talking about steak reminds me of one of the great steak restaurants of New York, Downey's Steak House on 43rd Street and 8th Avenue. Nobody but Jim Downey could run a place like his famous restaurant. Being an Irishman, he is a natural diplomatist; but above all, he is a friend of all artists. With an uncanny understanding of what makes us tick. He listens to our troubles. Then we are led gently into the interior. Sometime later we can be found tucking in to one of his incredible T-bone steaks. He is no less at home in his box at the 'Big A' racetrack than conversing with actors at the bar of his friendly restaurant. The congenially cavernous tunnels of the Steak house with its Thirties' Celtic ornament and deeply-buttoned hide upholstery provided the appropriate setting for my drawing.

5 Dylan Thomas liked the White Horse Tavern on Hudson Street, maybe because it resembles the old alehouses of the East End of London. In the long afternoons when none but the faithful congregate, the Horse's variations on the theme of model horses suggest an equine funeral parlour with undertones of an unusual saddlery business on the side. But the Horse pulsates with life, and if there *are* dull moments, these can be welcome too . . .

6 Another New York Saloon of great character is Costello's on Third
Avenue. Here one quiet morning I made a drawing of Johnny
Gallagher, the right-hand man now that Mrs Costello's husband, the
renowned Tim Costello, is no more. Costello's was one of great literary
bars that established themselves after the repeal of Prohibition. Its
relaxed atmosphere still makes it a favourite haunt of writers and
journalists. Memorabilia include Hemingway's hat, H. L. Mencken's
walking-stick and an incised mural by James Thurber on the wall,
facing an elaborate bar-screen of a style defined by Jonathan Miller as
being unusually fine Thirties' Aztec.

7 Further up Third Avenue, at 94th Street, in the centre of the old Irish District, is Ma O'Brien's place. Don't forget to visit Ma O'Brien, said Brendan. 'That Brendan Behan,' she hissed, when I dropped by one day: 'He owes me one hundred dollars, which if you're a friend of his and a gennelman, you'll pay me.' I didn't admit to Brendan's debt but paid her for my drink, and watched her bird-like jump to reach the cash register. She is very tiny, and has to use a box to stand on. The movement is made in a matter of seconds.

8 I used to take the long subway ride to Coney Island for an occasional break from the cigar smoke of Manhattan. Here the hundreds of seafood and hot-dog bars offered a fantastic variety of national snackery chiefly German, Jewish, Italian and Chinese. Nathan's, who introduced the frankfurter to Coney Island, dominates. Here on Surf Avenue, with appetites driven to starvation point by the bracing Atlantic air, famished citizenry mill about, working their way through vast quantities of hamburger steak, frankfurter sausage, pizza and chow mein, washed down by an inexhaustible torrent of cold draught lager.

9 A century after Washington followed on the heels of the evacuating British Army, the Bowery was a street of flashy saloons, dime museums, pawn-shops and music-halls. To a certain extent it still is, except that the saloons are no longer so flashy, and TV has taken the place of the old music-halls.

10 But one remains—Sammy's Bowery Follies—Here you can imbibe
draught Guinness with oysters and listen to the old songs rendered
by troupers of the 'twenties. There was 'Baby' Sandra weighing
all of 18 stone but moving around like a queen. Once a star, she
sings the hits of the 'thirties with swinging resonance. As I drew
her portrait, a hand slowly edged toward a packet of cigarettes
lying on the table between us. Without moving her level gaze,
or batting an eyelid, her great right arm slammed down on the
impertinence. 'You *must* be a greenhorn,' she growled to a cringing
bum nursing his fingers.

11 P. J. Clarke's on 3rd Avenue in sharp contrast, is a worldly place,
where worldly men discuss matters of moment in an atmosphere
of mahogany, beefsteak, stout and cigars. 'It takes you right
back to the heart of Dublin,' said I, 'Into the Shelbourne you mean,'
said the barman. 'Only the shawlies' snug is missing,' I continued.
'Praise be to God,' replied the barman.

12 Which reminds me of the time I met my Three Fates at
Slattery's, in Capel Street, Dublin. Until very recently Slattery's
was a great meeting place for an endless variety of characters. The
battered heroic-faced shawlies assembled like the remnants of an
Amazon legion for their daily ration of 'plain'. In one of the great
high snugs which radiated from the bar like the spokes of an old
wagon wheel I found Mary Dignam and her two friends. We had
a round and they sat for me. A half-hour went by, then Mary rose
to look over my shoulder, watching me add the lines to her face.
I felt a warm resilient hand on my wrist, 'Spare the hand, yer
honour, I'm not yit in the grave.' Raucous laughter. Another
round followed.

Slattery's Capel Street

13 Alas, the interior of Slattery's is no more. One fine day in the
spring of 1964, it was ruthlessly demolished by a sadly misguided
proprietor who associates mahogany with 'one-pinters'. The snugs
and the great altar-piece of the bar came crashing down to make way
for a select lounge which he hopes will 'attract the bo'emian fringe'.
'I want a big car and holidays in Spain like the rest of 'em,' says he.

15 The prosperity that has hit Dublin with the force of a hurricane, threatens to leave the city bereft of its fine old saloons and theatres. A great many are left, but they are fast falling, and the victims have been the more interesting places. The old Theatre Royal has already gone to make way for a high office block. The Olympia awaits its fate.

On the other side of the Liffey another old bar lives out its last days. O'Meara's is an extraordinary specimen of *art nouveau,* the like of which I've never seen anywhere else. The exterior is dominated by a series of remarkable plaster figures which symbolize an Ireland of myth and reality; Hibernia looks at Daniel O'Connell and an elaborate top-piece reads 'Erin Go Bragh 1870.' The interior is small but as high as a theatre with a vast amount of blistered mirrored shelving and a huge black stove. The place will be pulled down to make way for an extension to the offices of the Dublin Corporation. Meanwhile, O'Meara's is a great place to have a quiet jar at the close of the afternoon. At this time, the regulars drop in, silently checking off the race results over their frothy pints. Then with a sigh, they leave to join their families.

16 The Royal Circle Bar, formerly the Cosmo Bar, is also to go. This is a bar rich in its associations with the Dublin music-hall. Walls are lined with bills and photographs from the old days. The few disorientated regulars drift in and out, giving it the feeling of a doomed old ship.

17 Another one is the Blue Lion, in Parnell Street, probably the nearest of the Nightown bars described by Joyce in *Ulysses*. The clientele includes a variety of characters from the troubled 'twenties. Among them I found Biddy Kelly, a small-time moneylender to the poor. Biddy aroused reluctant admiration for her raucous ballads. Her favourite 'Friends today, Judases tomorrer' is intoned in a wild strident voice with the edge of an old file.

Biddy Kelly.
Blue Lion

79

18 Neary's on the other hand, might be described as Irish Affluent.
Here the company is dominated by actors and might-as-well-
spend-it types whose affluence is contemptuously commented upon
by the ever present fringe of literary incorrigibles. This was Louis
MacNeice's favourite bar in Dublin. It has a vaguely sinister
atmosphere: An entrance reminiscent of a side-door to purgatory with
a fine pair of kinky black hands grasping great lanterns aloft to
illuminate the entry of the convivial.

Defeat of a Drinking Man

BY ALAN BRIEN

NE day in 1956, it reached the ears of the *Evening Standard* that Hemingway was in mid-Atlantic on the *Liberté*. And some officious desk-bound executive conceived the idea of sending me down to Plymouth to extract an interview as he passed within sight of the English shore. My journey down there was made miserable by the thought that I might have to scale some slippery, swinging rope-ladder, green with fear and sea-sickness, while the great man sneered from the bridge.

Needless to say, the operation which had been simply demonstrated in Shoe Lane by moving a nicotined finger across a tiny map of England turned out, when put into effect by a flesh-and-blood correspondent dealing with actual trains, motor-cars, boats and bureaucrats, to be an odyssey of snags and frustrations. Once in my compartment, I was seized with a fit of nervous amnesia and suffered from delusions that I should be going to Portsmouth or Southampton. The shipping line at Plymouth was shrouded in a pall of vagueness about the hour, or even the day, of the *Liberté*'s arrival. Some officials promised that I could travel out to its mooring spot on the luggage tender. Others insisted that the Customs authorities would not permit any visitors. The shore-to-shore radio telephone operator connected me with a laconic American voice which insisted that Mr Hemingway had failed to turn up in time for the departure from New York.

My only success was in hiring a miniature tug affair, steered by a Bogartian, unshaven salt in plimsolls and a yachting cap, for five pounds. That at least would give a professional look to my expense sheet. We seemed to spend hours circling the ship

while the suitcases spilled out of some hole in its side like giant children's bricks, but no one resembling the great man peered out from among the faces along the rails. Once inside, not up a rope-ladder but across an almost equally vertiginous and shuddering ramp, I realised that I had not the faintest idea of where to start looking. It had never occurred to me that a liner could be so enormous and complicated—it was like being insinuated into the base of a bee-hive and told to have a word with the queen.

My deadline, which had once seemed so comfortingly distant, was now almost upon me. I started running the corridors shouting, 'Où est Monsieur 'Emingway? S'il vous bloody plaît.' Various steward figures in dazzling white ducks gave me cabin numbers, apparently at random, in French, and I plunged, sweating and Medusa-haired, into various wrong staterooms.

Twice I found bars tucked away in windowless metal caverns. The bar tenders denied any knowledge of 'Emingway and suggested different bars. Other journalists, who must have been deposited aboard by submarine, appeared at the end of long carpeted vistas, pantomimed fury like the Demon King and contempt for rival papers, and made off at a trot.

Eventually, having traversed the ship a couple of times, I arrived back at one of the bars and discovered there a battered, burly figure humped on a stool. He didn't look like Hemingway as much as like an old, over-exposed, badly retouched photograph of Hemingway. His hair and beard seemed to have been knitted on heavy wooden needles out of shiny, new, delicate barbed-wire. His face, such of it as was visible, was as bright as a peeled orange. And as he spoke tiny vessels appeared to explode across his cheeks like Very shells over a battlefield. 'Mr Hemingway,' he said, 'has nothing to say to the press, but I will buy you a drink.'

He spoke very slowly and carefully like someone counting out small change in a foreign currency and watching to spot the moment when he is being overcharged. I took the drink and poured it down into a stomach already distended by a queasy brew of ale and resentment. Now I was here I couldn't think of a single thing to say. A hasty rake over the surface of my mind produced a recent small news item—some bumptious tourist in Havana had taken Hemingway's place at a bar and been picked up and ejected by an indignant boozing crony. What was the use of Preaching about the True and the Beautiful and the Good and That's the Way It Should Be Among Men, I asked, if the preacher behaved like any Hollywood bum on a spree?

Hemingway punched himself in slow-motion on the ear as if annoyed that it should be transmitting such gibberish.

'You a drinking man?' he said.

'Yes,' I said.

'You have your favourite bar?'

'I suppose so,' I said.

'Then you have your favourite place in that bar. And that is your place. And they keep it for you.'

'No I don't,' I said, 'And no they don't.'

'Then it's not a real bar,' he said amicably. 'In a real bar, they keep your place where you put your back to the wall. That's all.'

'That's not all,' I said, stamping my feet. 'That's Warner Brothers gangster talk. How would you like it if I had you thrown out of my bar?'

Just then a fat Frenchman appeared. 'I think my seat, sir,' he announced.

Hemingway slid off like a boxer who hears the bell for the next round.

'Excuse me. Excuse *me*,' he said. 'Your seat, certainly.'

There was a longish pause and then we were both shaking with laughter until the counter rattled.

'To hell with newspapers,' he shouted. 'Come to France. We'll get off the boat and just drive into anywhere.'

I thought of the nicotined finger, the last edition, the pay slip, Lord Beaverbrook. 'Some other time,' I said. Back on shore I scribbled my newsless story as I waited for the call to FLE 3000 to come through. At last it came — 'the office is closed for the day,' they said, 'try tomorrow morning.'

And that's the way it was.

An 1865 Victorian

ROCOCO

Grill Room and a 1905

ART NOUVEAU

City of London Public House

by Nicholas Taylor

The Café Royal Grill Room

HE gorgeous gilded Palace! Why, you would think that a piece of Versailles' famous Palace had been cut off and brought over to England, as the Elgin marbles had been brought from Athens to the British Museum. In vain you may search here for the so much abused English style of decoration, whether Queen Anne, or any thing you like. The Café Royal is purely French, regular Louis XIV kind of ornamentation. Every thing is French, even the roast beef of old England has quite a Parisian taste about it . . . as different to St James's Hall Restaurant, on the other side of the street, as Folkestone is to Boulogne.' This paean comes from *Nocturnal London,* a volume of disgruntled reminiscence by 'A Late Secretary of Legation to the Court of St James's,' published in 1890. He was a Frenchman, and the Café Royal to him was an oasis in a foggy desert. Sir Herbert Beerbohm Tree, by contrast, once remarked that, 'If you want to see English people at their most English, go to the Café Royal, where they are trying their hardest to be French.'

There has in fact always been a certain ambivalence in the Café's Frenchness. It celebrates this year the centenary of its opening in Glasshouse Street on 11 February, 1865, by Daniel Nicolas Thévenon (1833-97), a bankrupt Paris wine merchant on the run from justice, who changed his name to Daniel Nicols, and later to Daniel de Nicols, when he built at Surbiton a palatial country house (now demolished), with a deer park. He died worth £600,000.*

When at the end of 1865 he bought a tailor's shop at 68 Regent Street (still the Café's address), he moved at once from the closed world of exiled poverty to the centre of London's fashionable elegance. His was not the first French *café-restaurant* in London —there were earlier examples such as Gatti's at the Adelaide

---

*For most of the historical facts in this article I am indebted to the book, *Café Royal,* by Guy Deghy and Keith Waterhouse, published in 1955, and also to Mr Deghy personally. I am also grateful to the Café's general manager, Mr Mervyn Cherrington, for his help. N.T.

Gallery and Evans's Supper Rooms at Covent Garden; but he made French cooking a central feature of the new broad-minded gaiety of London society under the leadership of the Prince of Wales (Edward VII). The environment of eating was almost as important for this as the quality of cooking. Nicols chose as his architects the then unknown partnership of Archer and Green, who designed almost everything for the Café Royal in the years 1865-85 (with a decorator named R. Lloyd, it seems).

During these twenty years Nicols gradually bought up the surrounding property so that, although his Regent Street entrance was comparatively narrow, there was a long side front in Air Street (Nos. 6-14) and a long back front in Glasshouse Street (Nos. 11-23). Within this irregular but compact block there were many rooms: the Grill Room on the ground floor along Air Street, the Domino Room next to it in the centre of the site with a back exit to Glasshouse Street, the Restaurant on the first floor reached by an imposing horseshoe-shaped staircase of marble, then two further floors of private banqueting rooms, culminating in a richly decorated Masonic Hall in the rooftop. These different rooms carefully reflected the variety of the clientele, from the artists and exiles in the Domino Room (the famous Café of Wilde and Beardsley and Augustus John) to the *salon privés* upstairs where young aristocrats entertained their lady friends, from the superb French *cuisine* in the Restaurant to the temporal splendour of the Masonic Hall (the Prince of Wales was a keen Mason, so this was a shrewd addition to Nicols's amenities).

The Grill Room, after the rebuilding of Regent Street and subsequent refurbishing, is now the only part of the Café Royal substantially in its original form. The rebuilding (1923-8) was carried out by the nondescript Henry Tanner behind the façade of Sir Reginald Blomfield's 'not too French, French' Quadrant. The Grill Room changed places with the Domino Room and was reduced in size. It was originally entered mainly from the Glasshouse Street side, the façade of which was illustrated in the *Building News* for 1873 with evident approval for its precise classical proportions and frilly balconies. The interior décor of the new Grill Room is in fact that of the old Domino Room, reduced in height and with certain features removed, such as the hanging electroliers and the great Corinthian columns of iron with their spiral swags. Thus the old haunt of Wilde, Beardsley, John, Dowson and other artists and poets has been transmogrified from an informal drinking place to a formal dining-room (the manager in the 1920s, Capt. Daniel Pigache, Nicols's grandson, had little sympathy with the artists). In the well-known paintings of the Domino Room by Orpen, Ginner and Allinson and in the descriptions by Beerbohm and Sitwell, most of the details of the present Grill Room can be seen, including the ceiling. The reduction in height has resulted in the caryatids now being somewhat over-sized in proportion to the room; on the other hand, much of the original 'height' was only in the artists' imaginations. The new ensemble, although to purists a 'phoney', fits together convincingly, and is possibly unique as an example of Victorian preservation in the 1920s.

The first impression, (1), is truly French: elaborate, formal and gay. The room is long, but the narrowness is counteracted by a firm division into three, apparently symmetrical, bays. There is a strong rhythm of mirrors and coupled termini caryatids, of blue urns and green cornices, of red plush chairs and benches and engraved glass screens, all picked out in lavish gilding. The Second Empire conventions are sustained in the constant use on plates and cutlery of the letter N and the Bonaparte crown—a trade mark of the Café foisted on the Royalist Nicols by his Bonapartist nephew, Georges Pigache, who is supposed to have told him innocently that the N stood for Nicols. The curtained 'windows' at the Glasshouse Street end form a strong conclusion to the room. Walk to that far end, look back, (2), and the impression is wholly different: not merely the infinite space of mirrors and lights, but—and this is where the Franco-British ambivalence comes in—the totally irregular shape, the informal confusion of diagonally placed walls and unequally spaced ceiling patterns. At once the caryatids cease to be the imperial handmaidens of the third Napoleon and become yet another High Victorian variation on the powerful busted Jacobean mermaids of the great screens at Hatfield and Andley End. Even the mirrors seem to have a touch of Gothic in their rounded, slightly cusped corners. It is this ambiguity—the constant change from formality to informality, from Garnier's Beaux-Arts discipline to the loosest Victorian naturalism—that makes this interior so stimulating and completely representative of the 'mainstream' of Victorian secular architecture.

The individual bays, (3), are formal enough. The mirrors (in this case, of the imitation-window type, with wavy gold-tasselled red curtains) are separated in bays by the termini caryatids in pairs. They dominate the Grill Room as surely as once also they did the Brasserie. They are fine, strapping young ladies, suggesting appropriately that good looks are not incompatible with good nourishment. Their flesh is a slightly sunburned off-white, their nipples are as unmarked as the Beaverbrook Press could wish, and cartouches with oval paintings of red and green flowers cover the delicate transition from generous hip to tapered pilaster. The pilaster ornament of golden flowers and acanthus leaves on a green background culminates in the gorgeous garlands of roses (light blue, pink, yellow, green), which the ladies hang by their powerfully flexed arms from their upswept coiffure.

In turn they support a richly modelled entablature . . . or do they? More than a moment's glance at the frontispiece will reveal the architects' Mannerist caprice which has placed the weight of the architrave on a shapeless mass behind the ladies' shoulder-blades and thus released their heads for the more feminine, more voluptuous task of holding the garlands and inclining their gaze towards the diners beneath. The entablature is brought forward over each caryatid and crowned by a bright blue urn with swags of flowers against a frieze of golden lattice work with a green background. Finally there is a powerful and rather coarse cornice, striped in gold and white panels. All this is incorrect in detail, no doubt, but it is formal. It is the combination of irregular spacing and a lavish provision of mirrors which causes the overall effect of Baroque, and almost Gothic, particularly in the riotous pile-up in each corner, (4).

The ceiling similarly is convincingly French in its Rococo framing of still-life paintings, (5). There is a different, though apparently symmetrical, composition of panels in each bay. However, the irregular shape of the room is only partially masked by the use of gold-on-green lattice work (similar to the frieze below) in irregular, almost amoeboid shapes, right in (5). The lattice work imparts a constant sense of flow away from the real focal points through the mirrors to the 'imaginary' focal points beyond. Forming the centrepiece of the four flower panels in each of the two end bays is a much larger frame containing a voluptuous scene of a goddess with attendant *amorini*, (6), playing instruments and holding flowers, with birds and beasts and clouds. In the centre there are three of these panels. Each scene is different. The goddesses have colossal thighs and hips (perhaps a similar fixation on the bottom to that of fashionable clothes of that date). The painter is supposed to have been an Italian, who worked at the Café on Sundays and at Nicols's country seat (Regent House, Surbiton) on weekdays. These paintings are a telling illustration that Victorian 'respectability' cannot be appreciated fully without the exuberant sensuality that went with it.

The overwhelming impression of the Grill Room is its feeling for space. It is in fact quite a small room (58 ft. by 26 ft.), but the sense of infinity, which is so often thought to be peculiar to modern architecture, transforms it into the sort of bourgeois Elysium portrayed in Offenbach's operettas. The endless caryatids and the confusion of interlocking polygons, (7), are enhanced by the survival of the original foliated sconces for the light fittings and the original gilded iron screens, with golden fabric and engraved glass. Three of these screens enclose the servery and cashier's desk, (8).

The architectural influence of the Café Royal was considerable. In 1870 the architectural competition for the Criterion, on the opposite side of Piccadilly Circus, was won by the young Thomas Verity with an exuberantly French Empire design (since sadly mutilated). In 1884 Verity was employed by Daniel Nicols as architect for his other enterprise, the Empire Theatre, Leicester Square, which had an all-gold foyer and a crimson-and-gilt interior, (rebuilt by Verity's son and later entirely remodelled for the present cinema). Archer and Green themselves designed the Holborn Restaurant (1883-5) and used their Anglicised Empire style in Cambridge Terrace at Regent's Park (1875), Attenborough's in Fleet Street (1883), the Hyde Park Hotel (1888) and—their most famous work—Whitehall Court (1884), which brings to the Westminster skyline the same uninhibited *joie-de-vivre* as in the Café Royal.

Verity and Archer and Green inspired a whole generation of London theatre and restaurant design (and particularly the ephemeral décor of shops and showrooms). In the Holborn Restaurant extension (1894), Frascati's (1893)—both now demolished—the National Opera House (now the Palace Theatre, 1890), the Savoy Hotel (1889) and Simpson's-in-the-Strand (1903-4) T. E. Collcutt tempered this exuberance of foreign detail with his training under 'correct' Gothic architects. The Café Royal style even went back to the Continent—to the Café New York at Budapest and the Café Central at Vienna—and to America (the Algonquin at New York). Besides glamour, the Café Royal also represented comfort. Nicols, on the advice of the Marquess of Blandford, was one of the first proprietors to install electric light (Blandford's father, the Duke of Marlborough, had daringly installed it at Blenheim); and at the Empire, Leicester Square, there were 'hitherto unknown fire prevention devices.'

The Grill Room is now a precious survival. Artists and poets were given the poorly decorated Brasserie as a substitute for the Domino Room; this in turn was abolished in 1951. In its place there is now a Restaurant, where the food may be good but the décor is hopelessly trivial and suburban. The banqueting rooms upstairs, one of which, the Pompadour, preserves a Rococo ceiling from Archer and Green, are mainly in a subfusc neo-Georgian. The seventh-floor suites (Sheraton, Chinese-Chippendale, etc.) were designed by Terence Verity, great-grandson of the Criterion architect. The present proprietor, Mr Charles Forte, deserves much credit for his preservation and spotless upkeep of the Grill Room; it must be hoped that elsewhere he will be able to match the exuberance and sophistication of Daniel Nicols and his architects with the equivalent patronage of the younger designers of this generation.

The Black Friar

 URNE-JONES's unlikely kinsman, Stanley Baldwin, called William Morris 'a great, glorious, jolly, human being.' Yet Morris's conviviality—the hearty quaffing of ale which distinguishes him from many left-wing heroes—is less often expressed in his own work than in that of his followers, who enjoyed merry evenings at the Art Workers' Guild in Queen Square. Perhaps the only building in London where it can now be savoured fully is that extraordinary pub, the Black Friar at 174 Queen Victoria Street, EC4. An innocuous Italianate block of c.1863 was transformed into a luscious folk-fantasy in about 1905 by H. Fuller Clark, an otherwise unknown architect, and Henry Poole, the sculptor, who was Master of the Art Workers' Guild in 1906.

The client was a licensee named Alfred Pettitt. The result of their collaboration is a priceless work of art, now in the midst of an area 'ripe for development.' On one side is the new *Times* building, on the other is the hole left by last year's demolition of the red sandstone Hand in Hand Insurance Society (by Henry Dawson). The Black Friar should not only be preserved but should be carefully looked after; there are already ominous signs of pilfering and decay in the décor, which has lost some of the original sparkle. Its isolation from the main centres of Arts and Crafts (Chelsea, Kensington, Hampstead) makes it all the more vulnerable.

The Black Friar stands on a narrow triangular site, (1), backing on to the railway and overlooking the Blackfriars traffic crossing. The ground floor respectfully continues the mullion-transom grid of the three upper floors, with smooth courses of pink and grey granite and dressings of Portland stone. In detail, however, it displays the familiar chunky forms of English Art Nouveau: in the massive flanking piers of the segmental doorways, (2); in the neat arcaded vents to the cellar; above all, in the sculptural enrichment which offers some foretaste of the thrills within. The doorway next to the bridge, (3), has a mosaic tympanum of a black friar and two massive entablatures carved with beasts and devils. The deep mosaic fascia says 'Saloon Bar/174/The Black Friar/ 174/Brandies'. Small copper panels, (4), of pointing friars, some sober, some less sober, direct the visitor into the Saloon Bar down the alleyway to the left. (The panel shown in this photograph was stolen during the summer of 1964.) Curiously, the public and private bars on the main corner never received their decoration, except for a uniform cladding in strips of yellowish brown and green marble. The Saloon and Snack Bars, largely tunnelled in vaults beneath the railway, possess all the crammed delights of Poole's work.

Customers in the Saloon Bar, (5), can retire from the usual marble-topped bar to the deep, enriched fireplace recess, framed by a broad tripartite arch, which encloses corner seats. Within the general wall pattern of brown and green marble, the fireplace itself is surrounded by dark varnished wood. It has a copper canopy and firedogs surmounted by little devils; the red and green marble surround has a polished copper keystone; the over-mantel has a bronze bas-relief of singing friars entitled 'Carols' and is flanked by two friars' heads with swags representing

'Summer' and 'Winter.' There are two splendid gas lamp brackets of copper, (6). The wooden wall clock nearby has a bronze relief of two monkeys playing musical instruments and the inscription, 'Tone Makes Music.' In the entrance wall is a stained glass window of a benevolent friar in a sunlit, walled garden.

Dominating the room are two large bronze bas-reliefs. Over the bar, (7) and (8), above the caption 'Tomorrow will be Friday,' five friar fishermen hand in a catch of trout and eels to six other greedily expectant friars. Over the three richly marbled arches to the Snack Bar, (9), is 'Saturday Afternoon,' an equally graphic portrayal of nine friar gardeners, whose produce—grapes, melon, onions, roses—is enamelled in realistic colours.

Because the ceiling is a disappointingly ordinary beam and plaster layout, the Saloon Bar fails to cohere. The Snack Bar, however, is a complete jewel house, (10). The three-bay barrel vault, on its gold, white and black mosaic, has large geometrical medallions and copper friars' heads. Against the end walls are two bronze reliefs: 'Don't advertise, tell a gossip' with a group of friars doing the weekly wash, and 'A good thing is soon snatched up,' with friars pushing a trussed pig in a wheelbarrow. Four little painted devils, representing music, drama, painting and literature, perch on the cornices below, (11).

The side walls are an incredible display: ten blocks on the cornice illustrating nursery rhymes; sixteen smaller capitals showing scenes from Aesop's Fables (a frog attacking a mouse, a snake with a sword in its mouth); nicely lettered mottoes such as 'Haste is slow' and 'Finery is foolery'; and four fantastic lamp brackets with alabaster figures of Morn, Even, Noon and Night holding up a bronze friar with water buckets. Best of all is the extra recess at one end, (12), containing a splendid relief of a gross, paunchy, sleeping friar, surrounded by Lilliputian fairies, one with mother-of-pearl wings. The 'window' below, with red marble colonnettes, is merely an arrangement of mirrors. This tunnel-like room is artificially lit throughout; the ventilation holes are boldly expressed on the end walls.

The Black Friar is genuine pop art of its time. The Arts and Crafts admiration for the hand-carved bestiaries of misericords is combined with parody on an intimate scale of all the current raves: the Byzantine splendours of mosaic taught in Lethaby's book; the gross exploitation of marble typical of Harry Wilson; the mother-of-pearl butterfly pinned to a marble wall (Whistler);

niches and mirrors derived from Leonard Stokes; swags and cherub-heads (neo-Wren); the combination in 'Carols' of exotic landscape (Italy) with the type of musical instruments used in English country churches in c.1800 (Cecil Sharp).

The real success of the Black Friar is that, like the best contemporary coffee bars, it reinforces vividly the popular prejudices of its customers. The decorative theme was chosen by Pettitt and Poole because the pub stands on the site of the City's medieval Dominican church. They then exploited the love-hate relationship between ordinary Protestant Britons and the Roman Church. It is the same suspicious fascination with Rome that is shown in Browning's 'Soliloquy of the Spanish Cloister' and in the extraordinary vogue for 'Cardinal' paintings, in which gorgeous redcloaked prelates were seen scheming and gossiping and enjoying such fruits as celibacy still afforded. The same line in Chaucerian comedy—the knowing grins, the vast paunches (in bas-relief!)—is pursued relentlessly by Poole in the Black Friar, which is probably the only pub of its type in the country. The reason for its uniqueness is of course that breweries and licensees were philistines; the Arts and Crafts patrons were usually the 'progressives,' who believed in temperance reform and preferred to build coffee houses (such as Sir Ernest George's at Newark and Sir Thomas Jackson's at Sevenoaks).

POSTSCRIPT

This article was hampered by the fact that both Fuller Clark, the architect, and Poole, the sculptor, were long dead and that I was unable to contact the Pettitt family. Since writing it, however, I have met Mr A. T. Bradford, an 89-year-old architectural sculptor who still has a flourishing practice in Southwark. He tells me that, while my date of c.1905 (on stylistic grounds) is probably correct for the Saloon Bar, the Snack Bar under the railway was not constructed until 1919-24 (there is an article on it in *The Architects' Journal* for 9 January, 1924). Although Poole did the major reliefs and the lamp brackets, Bradford's firm, E. J. and A. T. Bradford, carved most of the other ornaments in the Snack Bar—the capitals with Aesop's Fables, the cornice blocks with the nursery rhymes, the inscriptions and the mosaic work. It is remarkable that the authentic vitality of the Arts and Crafts Movement was sustained at such a late date.

According to Mr Bradford, H. Fuller Clark was a poor, hard-working assistant in the architect's department of one of the 'Big Five' banks (almost certainly Barclay's). His work for Alfred Pettitt was done 'on the side' (hence his obscurity). He also designed a gravestone at Wivenhoe, Essex, carved by Mr Bradford in memory of Pettitt's niece, Alice Hibbs, who died in 1923. I have recently discovered what I think was Pettitt's first commission for Henry Poole. In the central precinct of Brompton Cemetery is a tall stone obelisk, with a finely cut inscription and a statue (of an angel or muse) in bronze, to the memory of Alfred Pettitt's wife, who died in 1896 aged 38. Stylistically, this seems likely to be Poole's work. Alice Hibbs was Pettitt's companion after his wife's death.

Partly as a result of the publication of this article in the *Architectural Review*, the present owners of the Black Friar, Clarke Baker & Co., who are keen to preserve it, have cleaned and repainted the exterior. In current plans for the Blackfriars area, the building has been reprieved, but it may be in danger again after the 1967 traffic census.

CAFÉ ROYAL

1.   The first impression is truly French

2.   Walk to the far end, look back . . .

3. The individual bays are formal enough

4. . . . the riotous pile-up in each corner

5. The ceiling is . . . French in its Rococo framing of
   still-life paintings

6.   . . . in each of the two end bays . . . a goddess
     with attendant *amorini*, playing instruments
     and holding flowers, . . .

7. The endless caryatids and the confusion of interlocking

    polygons . . . enhanced by the . . . original

    sconces and gilded iron screens

8. Three of these screens enclose the servery
    and cashier's desk

BLACK FRIAR

1.   . . . a narrow triangular site

2.   . . . the familiar chunky forms of English Art Nouveau . . .

3.   The Queen Victoria Street entrance

under the railway viaduct

4, 5.　. . . pointing friars . . . direct the visitor to the Saloon Bar (below)

6.   . . . splendid gas lamp brackets of copper

7, 8.   Dominating the room are two large

bronze bas-reliefs

TO-MORROW WILL BE FRIDAY

9. 'Saturday afternoon' . . . nine friar gardeners . . .

10.   The Snack Bar . . . is a complete treasure house

11, 12.   . . . the extra recess at one end . . . and its ceiling

A Soldier of Fortune

A STORY — BY ALAN PRYCE JONES

HEN the Hungarian revolution broke out, I was still an undergraduate. It was my first experience of faces red with suppressed energy and fists thumping tables, of committee meetings and fund-raisings. Several friends of mine were organizing help for the freedom fighters. Passionate afternoons were spent in little bed-sitting rooms, discussing how best to get hold of arms, whether to talk to quartermasters or to raid barracks. We hoped to equip an ambulance and drive it to Budapest; to set up an underground broadcasting station; to do our bit. The misty November gathering in the quadrangle was dispelled by the fierce urge to be in the streets, crouching in the rubble of the cellars with the black-jacketed rebels whose smudgy pictures appeared in the newspapers. If we read books, it was not for our weekly essays, but to learn of Kossuth or the Hungarian Commune. Ordinary talk was loaded with calls to action culled from the heroic past. Most of us too, had done our national service, had seen the flags waving in the butts above the wooden targets, had doubled in the platoon attacks over countless heather moors. Suez, the contemporary crisis, was forgotten. Like an episode from the nineteen-thirties, it belonged to Eden, Munich and Hitler. Hungary was for the young.

Disregarding the university authorities, a few undergraduates did manage to get themselves to Hungary. They were the more adventurous or the more foolhardy. The others, myself included, continued to meet, to argue, to thump tables, sit on committees. There were exams ahead though, and small parochial tensions crept insidiously over the resounding issue which was resolved so suddenly and painfully that it seemed to cut us short while we were still debating whether to hurry out there or not. Even those who did reach Hungary before the collapse of the insurgents were too

R I C H A R D the *F I R S T,* King of
England, &c. called *Cœur de lion.*

T Hrough the Almighty's mercy and his aid,
   Jerufalem I conquer'd and fet free;
The Turks *and* Saracens, *who wast it laid,*
   I forced from Judea foon to flee.

The Isle of Cyprus *was subdu'd by me,*
   Sicily trembled at my Courage bold,
King Tancred *bought his Peace, and did agree,*
   To pay me Threefcore ounces of pure Gold,
Whilst I abroad won Honour many ways,
   Ambitious John, *my Brother, vext my Realm.*
In Auftria *I was Pris'ner many days.*
   Thus Floods of Troubles did me overwhelm.
     At length I home return'd, my ransom paid,
     But foon my Glory in the Grave was laid.

late to be any effective use. But their example made us feel a little sheepish. Especially as we also had to contend with the patronizing manner of those who had been maddeningly right all along, assuring us that anything students could do was unimportant and retrogressive. When the returning volunteers were plagued by the university authorities and later failed their exams into the bargain, our enthusiasm was finally deflated. The misty November turned into a cold December; and into the wintry struggle to lay the basis for so many future careers. The newly-formed club to discuss Hungarian affairs continued to meet until it became very familiar with the exploits of its four adventurer heroes. Every week too, the club contributed a few pounds to the fund for refugees. The atmosphere in the quadrangle was studious and subdued.

Laying the basis of my career though, did no good to my conscience. Counter-revolutionary agents, Fascist plots, I read it all

Dürnstein Castle and King Richard I

up in the Press and was increasingly dissatisfied. Success in the exams seemed incidental. Without saying a word to anyone, I bought a ticket to Vienna, and as soon as the vacation started, I discreetly set off.

It was already spring in Vienna. There was a sense of breaking out of a long hibernation, an English tortoise pushing up through dreary sand. With exhilaration I walked from the station, along the shuttered streets to the only address I had. It was the head-quarters of the Students' League for Freedom, an anomalous group that had grown of its own unexplained accord and with which our committee had corresponded, and indeed to which it had contributed its weekly pounds.

The league's offices were in the Schubertring, a wide sweeping boulevard which encloses Vienna's fashionable district. The ground floor of the building was occupied by a famous international com-pany, and it made me check the address which I had been given. Plate-glass and pile-carpets were inappropriate. Like most things in Vienna, however, it had another aspect. Pushed through enough swing-doors by a snub-nosed secretary, I was shown into a courtyard as dark and as stifling as a lift-shaft. Four floors up a thin wooden staircase was an opening on the landing. It was a mystery how office furniture could have been heaved up there, to this bolt-hole hardly bigger than a rabbit-hutch. But it was a heartwarming joke that this cramped headquarters should share its address with a world-wide trademark.

Philip ran the office. The arrival of strangers with suitcases was obviously part of the day's work to him. He was one of those people who can do about five things at once, with a mind so clearly compartmented that he could come to a decision of policy while speaking on a telephone about an organisational matter and writing a letter. He was a student of philosophy at the Sorbonne, although he must have been of Hungarian origin for he spoke the language faultlessly. He liked his name to be pronounced with an English accent. I never could find out anything more about him, because he had the knack of turning any personal question into a discussion of ideas. Philip was a born administrator, wonderfully equipped to be one of those mythical French civil servants who are alleged to combine intellectual gifts with impassivity and hard work. In about ten minutes I found myself running through a file to check the names of refugees who had come through the office against the general list of internees in temporary camps.

The frontiers were already closed and the exodus had now dwindled to a few isolated escapes. The border police had recovered the use of their blind eye. Philip seemed to have special powers though, for he was planning to drive to Budapest. Throughout the afternoon he harangued a series of officials in German, Hungarian and French. There was an office Land-Rover which he had used on earlier journeys and he was making sure that it was in order to make another expedition. His sallow thin face looked as if it had been fitted to the telephone. I was in Vienna for this sort of thing, and remembered the undergraduate emotions as if they were fragmented but prophetic dreams.

When Philip finally hung up, having fixed his journey, I asked him if he knew where I could stay. 'How long are you going to be in Vienna?' He picked up the file to see if I had been useful to him and ran his finger down my work. Although I knew that the summer term was due to start all too soon, I shrugged my shoulders. Philip decided. 'Come along with me.' Taking my suitcase, I followed him along corridors, up and down stairs, irregular and twisting, until I had lost all sense of direction. The building apparently ramified like a maze around its courtyard, consisting of several different constructions moulded into one great warren. Eventually he showed me into a bedroom with a particularly high, almost oblong, ceiling. 'You can share this with Dini,' he said. The room made a very old-fashioned impression; two vast brass bedsteads smothered by humpbacked eiderdowns, an upholstered chair or two, an incongruous potted palm-tree, draped plum-coloured curtains. When I turned round, Philip had already gone.

It took me several days to find my bearings. The whole building belonged to a rich banker with political leanings. Most of it was let to respectable tenants like the electrical combine on the ground floor, but this flat and some spare rooms and the little office had been given free to the league. Philip had arranged it. Although I became familiar with the narrow corridors from my bedroom to the office, there was a more dignified entry up the main staircase. There was nothing conspiratorial about this, so we preferred to use the back way. My room-mate Dini, though, always went round to the front stairs and he would make a show of walking up the stone flights. The first week was spent largely in trying to understand why this was so important to him, for it was typical of the man.

Gesture was everything to Dini. Performance counted for nothing. Not that he was lazy. Anybody could tell from his appearance that his gaunt figure contained a good deal of surplus energy. He looked rather like an eighteenth-century aristocrat, with a face resembling a woodcock's, thin and beaky, generally inclined to one side. His lively eye shone all the brighter for his nearly bald head. He seemed to flutter when he walked, as if he wanted to put himself out, to go the shortest distance by the longest route. I could never master his surname. It looked like doodling on a typewriter, for it was a chain of consonants. It doesn't matter much either, for now that he is in New York, I'm sure it has a simpler Anglo-Saxon form. Dini was one of the first to leave Hungary, almost the instant the revolution broke out. It didn't take long to discover the facts: unlike Philip, Dini loved talking about himself. The son of a peasant, he had drifted into an industrial town where he worked his way up to become a foreman of a flour mill. It had been child's play to supervise because it was automated. Easy job: high production: he told it all a hundred times. One day he had fallen asleep at his work. Sacked immediately he had joined the army and been promoted driver to the colonel of his regiment. But the colonel was only twenty-four —exactly Dini's age—and the nephew of a high-up, so Dini had been free-spoken. It was none too soon when Dini walked into the league's office on the Schubertring.

This information was directed at me through the greater part of our office hours, and lasted well into the night. Philip left for Budapest the morning after my arrival and Dini was therefore my only guide. Office routine stopped with Philip's departure. People drifted in and out, there was a girl typing letters in the morning, and refugees coming to ask favours of Dini from time to time. We spent a large part of every day in the various consulates— American, British, Canadian—trying to arrange visas and interpret immigration laws. Dini and I acted as a team. We both spoke German reasonably well and the consular staffs were even helped by our presence. In spare moments I had to give Dini English lessons because he was preparing for his American onslaught. Broker, bills of exchange, double entry, those were the kind of words with which he wanted to be familiar. We usually spent a bit of the lesson reconstructing the processes of Wall Street from the daily financial news items. Dini knew what lay ahead.

The days passed quickly enough. Only one incident was beyond our control. The office was invaded early one morning by a fully armed Swiss soldier. Reservists in Switzerland, he explained, always kept their equipment at home, down to field rations, arms and ammunition. An impulse had suddenly seized him, and here he was, demanding to be despatched immediately to the front line. In the end we had to give him the name of a small town on the Austrian border, and then we crept down the back stairs to watch him go marching away. Otherwise we managed to fix up the evacuation of some of the refugees on our lists, sending them by chartered bus to Munich from where they were flown out to the New World. Philip had arranged all this as well, or more probably, I suppose, had convinced the authorities and the consulates that he could help them. I was never in a position to understand Philip's influence, and of course Dini discounted it. So we loafed about Vienna, sitting in bars with scores of Hungarians who crowded round Dini. We walked the streets and stretched out on the park benches. It was a full, fresh spring, bathed with limpid sunlight and with blossom on the fruit trees as heavy as snow. I had been born in Vienna, as a matter of fact, and one afternoon I took Dini to see the house. It was the first time I'd been there since I was a baby, but what could I say? We circled it, talking of bulls and bears.

When Philip came back unexpectedly, there was the inevitable row. Fortunately it took place in Hungarian. Philip accused us of idleness, and Dini apparently answered that Philip didn't know how to delegate authority. The outcome suited both of them. Philip got to work—and Dini was to report the next day to the transit camp at Eisenstadt so that his departure to America could be speeded up. I admired Philip enormously: his passions were effective. Meanwhile, he thrust a vast amount of paper work at me, and I only finished it for him by staying in the office until the small hours.

As a farewell offering Dini was allowed to borrow the Land-Rover and I was to accompany him. Histrionically he kissed Philip and the girl typist and insisted on going downstairs to shake hands with some of the staff of the electrical company. It was as if he was setting out from his estates on a Grand Tour.

'I won't drive out of Vienna to the east,' he said, taking the wheel, 'we'll make a big circuit.' So we rattled off in the wrong direction, down the valley of the Danube, pushing through the dreary Viennese suburbs built in aggressively proletarian colonies as if defying any other part of the city to mix in with them. 'It's funny to think you and I might have belonged to this Austro-

Hungarian empire,' said Dini, 'and now we're playing at Anglo-Saxons. What are they really like?' And as usual with Dini, he answered his own questions, going off into the multiple corridors of his imagination.

The road took us into the country. There was no point arguing with Dini that Eisenstadt lay in the opposite direction. Instead we arrived at the great baroque abbey of Melk, magnificently dominating a bend of the Danube. Accelerating as fast as he could, Dini screwed off the road under an ornate arch and bumped the Land-Rover into an exterior courtyard. The abbey opened up before us in a series of further courtyards and archways, successively more spacious and florid, culminating in the architectural triumph of the church set against the view of the river. Because it was falling into disrepair, Dini was prepared to allow its splendour. 'I'd hate it if it was rich,' he said darkly. He poked into the sacristy, the chapels, the old library. I began to wonder if he intended the journey to be an obscure insult to Philip. Perhaps he would refuse to go to Eisenstadt, and I would have to drive him ignominiously home.

We set off down the river valley, through little rustic villages, orchards, vineyards with their blackened and twisted vines, the almost operatic Danubian countryside, as pretty as in a fairy story. We stopped at Schonbühel with its towering rock and its aura of feudalism, and we stopped again at Dürnstein. All the fruit trees were in flower and Dini insisted on going for a walk to admire them. He was impressed to discover that Richard Lionheart had been imprisoned in the fortress of Dürnstein before paying his ransom. It put him off the long climb up the mountain and instead we went down the hillside towards the river.

As we were leaving the village along a footpath, an old man stopped us. Would we like a glass of wine? He was the owner of a *Keller* and was inviting us in. Dini and he were arm-in-arm in a matter of minutes. We went down a long flight of stone steps, into the darkness of the cellar. It took some time to get accustomed to the surroundings. We introduced ourselves formally, peering in the half-light. The two sons and a daughter were already working in the cellar and there were two friends helping them. Ceremoniously we were shown to stone seats running round three sides of a room, while one of the sons drew some wine out of an enormous barrel. Its cold taste corresponded to the chill of the underground room. We drank carefully. Dini was immediately at ease. I found it very difficult to understand the old man's

German, for he spoke with a broad peasant accent. But very soon Dini was launching out: the mill, asleep at his job as foreman, the colonel's driver. The revolution.

They asked him about the uprising. Before Dini could answer, though, we were all taken down a passage in the cellar, past a long row of barrels and casks, in order to fetch some better wine. Standing stiffly in front of us, under the high vaulted roof, the old man delivered a brief lecture about the difference in quality. First we tasted it, as it was drawn off, and then the son filled a jug. When we returned to our seats, Dini was allowed to hold the floor. I heard once again the account of his walk from Budapest to Vienna, and I admired his consistency. He told the story well and it was the same story. By the time he had finished, the jug was empty. We trooped off to another part of the cellar to try a fresh vintage.

I am a light drinker as a rule, and rather an undiscriminating one, so that most of the conversation about *Auslese* and *Heuriger* was lost on me. Dini took to it as if he had been a wine-grower all his life, although I doubt if he understood more of the dialect than I did. On me the wine had a crystallizing effect as if my temperature was slowly sinking. This corresponded to a clarification of the mind. Looking back, I think this was caused by the damp of the cellar, for when I have drunk above ground, as it were, I have never experienced this sensation of the mind freezing until everything extraneous was excluded. I imagine that Philip's mind is always in this state. Now I listened intently to Dini. He was explaining how his parents lived in Hungary, going into the daily details of their lives. They were asking him the price of meat, and what kind of harvest they had. Did they still grow wine? Dini had them spell-bound. It was an event, something they would remember, for they had never lived under the Russians. This provided first-hand evidence about what they had heard from third-hand sources inside the allied zones. Dini knew exactly what he was doing, sitting there calmly, gesticulating to make his points, nodding his woodcock's head. When he was fully in his stride, the party no longer had to be broken up to fetch more wine —one of the sons detached himself silently to fill the jug. The gritty, grapy smell of the cellar heightened the illusion that we were rehearsing a Guy Fawkes plot, or acting out a scene from *The Ring*. For it was the same kind of smell as the suggestive draught blowing across a theatre from the wings and the stage-sets.

The son leaving and returning with the single prop was a minor character taking an awkward cue.

The self-conscious celebrity brought the curtain down on himself. He was digressing into politics and he made a joke, referring to the new reading of the old Austrian *K.u.K.* as *Kaiser und Khrushchev*. It was a little too quick for his audience. The thread was broken, and Dini was too clever to spin another. Shrinking against the wall, he drew himself back into the shadows as if nervous all of a sudden that he had bored his hosts. The talk became general for a while until the old man went off to fetch what he called 'something special.' He filled our glasses and stood up on the stone bench to drink a toast to Dini, who quickly added his own conclusion, 'and to my success in America.' There was laughter. Then Dini proposed a toast to the old man, to his kindness in taking in strangers. The old man rubbed his hands together. It was the sign of dismissal: the family melted away into the network of passages and he escorted us to the door.

Outside the sunlight was so bright by contrast that it was as if I had been sandbagged. I could hardly bear to keep my eyes open. And the change in temperature was no less violent. It was a warm spring which came to loosen the frozen immobility of the cellar. To climb the hill, through the orchards at the foot of Richard Lionheart's fortress, was like returning through memories so long-forgotten that they had grown detached. I thawed, melting again into the prettiness of the village, blurring the sharp perceptions of the cellar. It was now a question of getting Dini to Eisenstadt without delay. This time I took the wheel.

We turned back down the road to Melk, before branching off into the country. Driving eastwards at last, I had satisfied Dini's whim by the great many unnecessary miles which we now had to cover. He was unnaturally silent, as if he had talked himself out in the cellar. Like a gutted candle, he drooped, lolling on the flat seat of the Land-Rover.

'You know,' I began, 'I saw it all plainly in that cellar. Perhaps because it was so unexpected to be invited in like that, or perhaps because it was so cold in there. I saw you, Dini, quite bald and rather fat, with a big jewelled ring on your finger, standing up at an endless row of civic lunches, the big fake words ringing out of your mouth, telling your fellow-citizens about liberty and the state and all the rest of it. And you'll leave these functions rather bloated, to cruise off to your stockbroker's office in a car about a

Lajos Kossuth, 1802-1884

hundred yards long. You're going to be awful in America, Dini.'

It revived him. 'Topp auf Topp, und Schlag auf Schlag,' he said, with some dim schoolboy recollection of *Faust* which he hoped would please me, I suppose. 'You know, you're absolutely right. I'm looking forward to it very much. I am very unwise. All Hungarians are unwise, they'd never have made that revolution if they weren't.'

'I'd go back if I were you,' I said. 'Philip could easily fix it. You'll get spoilt over there, you'll never be the same again.'

'So that's what we've come to, is it? What if there was nothing to spoil?'

'I just pictured you over there telling them about your experiences for ever and ever, year after year,' I said.

'Do you think they will really want to listen? But it was nice of you to come all the way from your snug little university just to tell me that. I'll make a bargain with you. If I'm unhappy in the States, I'll write to you and pour out my heart, and if you never hear from me, you'll know I've made it. And you'll know that you've done your bit.' Rather self-consciously I turned sideways, away from the steering-wheel and shook his hand. Uncomfortably too, I found myself remembering the way we had sat in the college and the images we had formed of the freedom-fighters. I gave him my address and out of the corner of my eye watched him write it down. 'The big gesture.' He was laughing.

In Eisenstadt, which we reached in the late afternoon, there is a palace which formerly belonged to the Esterhazy family. A board outside announced that it was open to the public, and on display were souvenirs of Haydn, a former musician to the family. Dini was excited, saying that he had once been to the principal Esterhazy castle in Hungary, now an agricultural college. He wanted me to stop, on the pretext that he ought to know about the past of great Hungarian nobles. When I refused because it was growing late and I had to return the Land-Rover to Philip, he came back at me: 'Yes, you must do your duty: Philip will be very angry if the refugees aren't shipped off smoothly. You are like all the English, you haven't got a sense of occasion. To the wholesale despatch centre, if you please.'

It was a fairly accurate description of the transit camp. A former Russian army barracks which had been largely dismantled, it was not equipped to hold several hundred refugees. There was only one tap in the whole compound, and only one receptacle capable of holding water; a rusty metal bath. Fortunately nobody was expected to live in these conditions for very long: people were only sent there when their passages abroad were guaranteed within the fortnight. There were no spare beds and I found Dini some straw, which we staked out under a window which still had glass in it. Then we reported to the camp office where he was issued with a mug and a spoon. Nobody paid much attention to a single new arrival.

'Goodbye,' said Dini, 'don't forget, you did your bit for the Hungarian revolution—in the cellar.' I was ashamed by his laughter.

Back in my college, the wisteria was just breaking into its bunches of heavy flowers under my windows. The university was charged with the energy of summer. The committee meetings of the previous winter had vanished with the fogs, and the Hungarian crisis was over, dead and forgotten—like last autumn's leaves. I told nobody that I had been to Vienna, and nobody asked. There has been no letter from Dini, not a word from that day to this. And not a line from Philip.

The Great Carp Ferdinand

A CHRISTMAS STORY

BY EVA IBBOTSON

HIS is a true story, the story of a Christmas in Vienna in the years before the First World War. Not only is it a true story, it is a most dramatic one, involving love, conflict and (very nearly) death—and this despite the fact that the hero was a fish.

Not any fish, of course: a mighty and formidable fish, the Great Carp Ferdinand. And if you think the story is exaggerated and that no fish, however mighty, could so profoundly affect the lives of a whole family, then you're wrong. Because I have the facts first-hand from one of the participants, the 'littlest niece' in the story, the one whose feet, admittedly, failed to reach even the first rung of the huge, leather-backed, silver-buttoned dining-room chairs, but whose eyes cleared the table by a good three inches so that, as she frequently points out, she saw it all. (She came to England, years later, this littlest niece, and became my mother, so I've kept tabs on the story, checked it for accuracy time and again.)

The role the great carp Ferdinand was to play in the life of the Mannhaus family was simple, though crucial. He was, to put it plainly, the Christmas Dinner. For in Vienna, where they celebrate on Christmas Eve and no one, on Holy Night, would dream of eating meat, they relish nothing so much as a richly-marinated, succulently roasted carp. And it is true that until you have tasted fresh carp with all the symphonic accompaniments (sour cream, braised celeriac, dark plum jam) you have not, gustatorily speaking, really lived.

But, the accent is on the word *fresh*. So that, when a grateful client with a famous sporting estate in Carinthia presented Onkel Ernst with a live twenty-pounder a week before Christmas, the Mannhaus family was delighted. Onkel Ernst, a small, bandy-legged man whose ironic sympathy enabled him to sustain a flourishing solicitor's practice, was delighted. Tante Gerda, his plump, affectionate wife, was delighted. Graziella, their adorable (and adored) eighteen-year-old daughter, was delighted, as was Herr Franz von Rittersberg, Graziella's 'intended', who loved his food. Delighted, too, were Tante Gerda's three little nieces, already installed with their English governess in readiness for the great Mannhaus Christmas, and delighted were the innumerable poor relations and rich godfathers whom motherly Tante

Gerda collected every Christmas Eve to light the candles on the great fir tree, open their presents and eat . . . roast carp.

Accommodation for the fish was not too great a problem. The house in Vienna was massive and the maids, simple country girls accustomed to scrubbing down in wooden tubs, cheerfully surrendered the bathroom previously ascribed to their use.

Here, in a gargantuan, mahogany-sided bath with copper taps the size of Niagara, the huge, grey fish swam majestically to and fro, fro and to, apparently oblivious both of the glory of his ultimate destiny and the magnificence of his setting. For the bathroom was no ordinary bathroom. French tea roses—marvellous, cabbage-sized blooms—swirled up the wallpaper, were repeated on the huge china wash bowl and echoed yet again in the vast chamber-pot—a vessel so generously conceived that even the oldest of the little nieces could have sunk in it without a trace.

And here to visit him as the procession of days marched on towards Christmas came the various members of the Mannhaus family.

Onkel Ernst came, sucking his long, black pipe with the porcelain lid. Not a sentimental man, and one addicted to good food, he regarded the carp's ultimate end as thoroughly fitting. And yet, as he looked into the marvellously unrevealing eye of the great, grey fish, admired the gently-undulating whiskers (so much more luxuriant than his own sparse moustache), Onkel Ernst felt a distinct sense of kinship with what was, after all, the only other

male in a houseful of women. And as he sat there, drawing on his pipe, listening to the occasional plash as the carp broke water, Onkel Ernst let slip from his shoulders for a while the burden of maintaining the house in Vienna, the villa in Baden-Baden, the chalet on the Wörther See, the dozen or so of Gerda's relatives who had quitted, really rather early, the struggle to support themselves. He forgot even the Juggernaut of bills which would follow the festivities. Almost, but not quite, he forgot the little niggle of worry about his daughter, Graziella.

Tante Gerda, too, paid visits to the carp—but briefly, for Christmas was something she could never trust to proceed even for a moment without her. She came hung about with lists, her forehead creased into its headache lines, deep anxieties curdling her brain. Would the tree clear the ceiling—or, worse still, would it be too short? Would Sachers send the meringue and ice-cream swan in time? Should one (really a worry, this) 'send' to the Pfischingers, who had not 'sent' last year but had the year before? (Oh, that terrible year when the Steinhauses had sent a basket of crystallized fruit at the very last minute, when all the shops were shut, and she had had to re-wrap the potted azalea the Hellers had sent and send it to the Steinhauses—and then spent all Christmas wondering if she had removed the label!)

Bending over the fish, Tante Gerda pondered the sauce. Here, too, was anxiety. Celeriac, yes, lemon, yes, onion, yes, pepper-corns, ginger, almonds, walnuts—that went without saying. Grated honeycake, of course, thyme, bay, paprika and dark plum jam. But now her sister, writing from Linz, had suggested mace . . . The idea was new, almost revolutionary. The Mann-haus carp, maceless, was a gastronomic talking-point in Vienna. There were the cook's feelings to be considered. And yet . . . even Sacher himself was not afraid to vary a trusty recipe.

The carp's indifference to his culinary environment was some-how calming. She closed her eyes for a second and had a sudden, momentary glimpse of Christmas as existing *behind* all this if only she could reach it. If she could just be sure that Graziella was all right. And she sighed, for she had never meant to love any-one as much as she loved her only daughter.

Franz von Rittersberg came, too, to see the carp. A golden-haired, blue-eyed, splendid young man, heir to a coal-mine in Silesia, the purpose of his visit was strictly arithmetical. He measured the carp mentally, divided it by the number of people expected to sit down to dinner, estimated that his portion as the future Mannhaus son-in-law was sure to be drawn from the broader, central regions—and left content.

And, escaping from the English governess, scuttling and twittering like mice, white-stockinged, brown-booted, their behinds deliciously humped by layers of petticoat, came the little nieces clutching stolen bread rolls.

'Ferdinand,' whispered the youngest ecstatically, balancing on the upturned, rose-encrusted chamber-pot. Her sisters, who could see over the sides of the bath unaided, stood gravely crumbling bread into the water. The fish was a miracle; unaware of them, yet theirs. *Real.*

(At night, each night, when the nursemaid left them, they tumbled out from under the feather bed and marshalled them-

selves for systematic prayer. 'Please God, make them give us something that's *alive* for Christmas,' they prayed night after night after night.)

But it was Graziella, the daughter of the house, who came oftenest of all. Perched on the side of the bath, her dusky curls rioting among the cabbage roses on the wall, she looked with dark, commiserating eyes at the fish. Yet, though she was by far the loveliest of the visitors, Ferdinand's treatment of her was uncivil. Quite simply, he avoided her. Carp, after all, are *fresh* water fish, and he had noticed that the drops which fell on him when she was there were most deplorably saline.

She was a girl the gods had truly smiled upon—loving and beloved; gay and kind, and her future as Frau Franz von Rittersberg was rosily assured. And yet each day she seemed to get a little thinner and a little paler, her dark eyes filling with ever-growing bewilderment. For when you have been accustomed all your life to giving, giving, giving, you may wake up one day and find you have given away—yourself. And then unless you are a saint (and even, perhaps, if you are) you will spend the nights underneath your pillow, trapped and wretched, licking away the foolish tears.

And so the days drew steadily on, mounting to their climax—Christmas Eve. Snow fell, the tree arrived, the last candle was lit on the Advent ring. The littlest niece, falling from grace, ate the chimney off the gingerbread house. The exchange of hampers became ever more frenzied. The Pfischingers, who had still not sent, invaded Tante Gerda's dreams . . .

It was on the morning of the twenty-third that Onkel Ernst and his future son-in-law assembled to perform the sacrificial rites on the great Carp Ferdinand.

The little nieces had been bundled into coats and leggings and taken to the Prater. Graziella, notoriously tender-hearted, had been sent to Rumpelmayers on an errand. Now, at the foot of the stairs, stood the cook, holding a gargantuan earthenware baking dish—to the left of her the housemaids, to the right the kitchen staff. On the landing upstairs, Tante Gerda girded her men—a long-bladed kitchen knife, a seven-pound sledgehammer, an old, slightly rusty sword of the Kaiser's Imperial Army which someone had left behind at dinner. . . .

In the bathroom, Onkel Ernst looked at the fish and the fish looked at Onkel Ernst. A very slight sensation, a whisper of premonition, nothing more, assailed Onkel Ernst, who felt as though his liver was performing a very small *entrechat*.

'You shoo him down this end,' ordered Franz, splendidly offhand. 'Then, when he's up against the end of the bath, I'll wham him.'

Onkel Ernst shooed. The carp swam. Franz—swinging the hammer over his head—whammed.

The noise was incredible. Chips of enamel flew upwards.

'Ow, my eye, my *eye*,' yelled Franz, dropping the hammer. 'There's a splinter in it. Get it OUT!'

'Yes,' said Onkel Ernst. 'Yes . . .'

He put down the sword from the Kaiser's Imperial Army and climbed carefully on to the side of the bath. Even then he was only about level with Franz's streaming, blue eye. Blindly, Franz thrust his head forward.

The rest, really, was inevitable. Respectable, middle-aged Viennese solicitors are not acrobats. They don't pretend to be. The carp, swimming languidly between the folds of Onkel Ernst's trousers, found, as he had expected, nothing even mildly edible.

It was just after lunch that Onkel Ernst, dry again and wearing his English knickerbockers, received, in a mild way, Guidance from Above.

It was all so easy, really. No need for all this crude banging and lunging. Simply, one went upstairs; one pulled out the plug; one went out, locking the door behind one. And waited . . .

A few minutes later, perfectly relaxed, Onkel Ernst was back in his study. He was not only holding the newspaper the right way up, he was practically *reading* it.

The house was hushed. Franz, after prolonged ministrations by the women of the family, had gone home. The little nieces were having their afternoon rest. The study, anyway, had baize-lined double doors. Even if there *were* any thuds—thuds such as a great fish lashing in its death agony might make—Onkel Ernst would not hear them.

What he did hear, not very long afterwards, was a scream. A truly fearful scream, the scream of a virtuoso, and one he had no difficulty in ascribing to the under-housemaid, whose brother was champion yodeller of Schruns. A second scream joined it, and a third. Onkel Ernst dashed out into the hall.

His first impression was that the hall was full of people. His second was that it was wet. Both proved to be correct.

Tante Gerda, trembling on the edge of hysteria, was being soothed by Graziella. The English governess, redoubtable as all her race, had already commandeered a bucket and mop and flung herself into the breach. Maids dabbed and moaned and mopped —and still the water ran steadily down the stairs, past the carved cherubs on the banisters, turning the Turkish carpet into pulp.

The inquiry, when they finally got round to it, was something of a formality since the culprits freely admitted their guilt. There they stood, the little nieces, pale, trembling, terrified—yet some-how not truly repentant-looking. Yes, they had done it. Yes, they had taken the key out from behind the clock, yes, they had unlocked the bathroom door, turned on the taps . . .

Silent, acquiescent, they waited for punishment. Only the suddenly-descending knicker-leg of the youngest spoke of an almost unbearable tension.

Graziella saved them, as she always saved everything.

'Please, Mutti? Please, Vati . . . So near Christmas?'

Midnight struck. In the Mannhaus mansion, silence reigned at last. Worn out, their nightly prayer completed, the little nieces slept. Tante Gerda moaned, dreaming that the Pfischingers had sent a giant hamper full of sauce.

Presently a door opened and Onkel Ernst in his pyjamas crept softly from the smoking room. In his hand was an enormous shotgun—a terrible weapon some thirty years old which had belonged to his father—and in his heart was a blood lust as violent as it was unexpected.

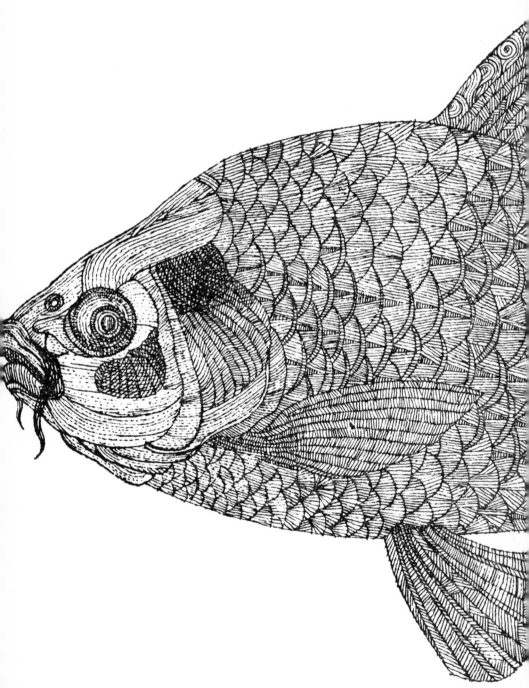

Relentlessly he climbed the stairs; relentlessly he entered the bathroom and turned the key behind him. Relentlessly he took three paces backwards, peered down the barrel—and fired.

Graziella, always awake these nights, was the first to reach him.

'Are you all right, Papa? Are you all right?'

Only another fearful volley of groans issued from behind the bolted door. Tante Gerda rushed up, her grey plait swinging. 'Ernst, *Ernst?*' she implored, hammering on the door. '*Say something, Ernst!*'

The English governess arrived in her Jaeger dressing-gown, the cook . . . Together the women strained against the door. It was hopeless.

'Phone the doctor, the fire brigade. Send for Franz, quick,' Gerda ordered. 'A man—we need a *man.*'

The governess ran to the telephone. But Graziella, desperate, threw her fur cape over her nightdress and ran out into the street.

Thus it was that in the space of half a minute the life of Sebastian Haffner underwent a complete and total revolution. One minute he was free as air, easy-going, a young man devoted to his research work at the University—and seconds later he was a committed, passionate fanatic ready to scale mountains, slay dragons and take out a gigantic mortgage on a house. For no other reason than that Graziella, rushing blindly down the steps into the lamplit street, ran straight into his arms.

Just for a fraction of a second the embrace in which Sebastian held the trembling girl remained protective and fatherly. Then his arms tightened round her and he became not fatherly—not fatherly at all. And Graziella, with snowflakes in her hair, looked up at the stranger's kind, dark, gentle face and could not—simply could not—look away.

Then she remembered and struggled free. 'Oh, please come,' she gabbled, pulling Sebastian by the hand. 'Quickly. It's my father . . . The carp has shot him.'

Instantly Sebastian rearranged his dreams. He would visit her regularly in the asylum, bring her flowers, read to her. Slowly, through his devotion, she would be cured.

'Hurry, please, please. He was groaning so.'

'The carp?' suggested Sebastian, running with her up the steps. 'My father. Oh, *come!*'

Maids moaned at the foot of the stairs. Tante Gerda sobbed on the landing.

Sebastian was magnificent. Within seconds he had seized a carved oak chair and begun to batter on the door. Quite quickly, the great door splintered and fell. At Sebastian's heels they trooped into the bathroom.

Onkel Ernst sat propped against the side of the bath, now groaning, now swearing, his hand on his shoulder, which was caked with blood. Round him were fragments of rose-encrusted china and shattered mirror which the lead shot ricocheting from the sides of the bath and grazing Onkel Ernst's shoulder, had finally shattered. The carp, lurking beneath the water taps, appeared to be asleep.

'Ernst!' shrieked Tante Gerda, and dropped on her knees beside him.

'Bandages, scissors, lint,' ordered Sebastian, and Graziella fled like the wind.

It was only a flesh wound, and Sebastian, miracle of miracles, was a doctor, though the kind that worked in a lab. Quite soon, Onkel Ernst, undisputedly the hero of the hour, was propped on a sofa, courageously swallowing cognac, egg yolk with vanilla, raspberry cordial laced with *kirsch*. The family doctor arrived, pronounced Sebastian's work excellent, stayed for cognac, too. The fire brigade, trooping into the kitchen, preferred *slivovitz*.

And upstairs, forgotten, seeing nothing but each other, stood Graziella and Sebastian.

This was it, then, thought Graziella, this wanting to sing and dance and shout and yet feeling so humble and so *good*. This was what she had never felt, and so had nearly thrown herself to Franz as one throws a bone to a dog to stop it growling . . . As if in echo to her thoughts, the bell shrilled yet again and Franz von Rittersberg was admitted. His eye was still swollen and his temper not of the best.

'This place is turning into a madhouse,' he said, running up the stairs. 'Do you know what time it is?'

Graziella did not. Time had stopped when she ran into Sebastian's arms. Years were to pass before she quite caught up with it again.

'Well, for heaven's sake let's finish off this blasted fish and get back to bed,' he said, shrugging off his coat and taking out a knife and a glass-stoppered bottle. 'I've brought some chloroform.'

'No!'

Graziella's voice startled both men by its intensity. 'In England,' she said breathlessly, 'in England, if you hang someone and it doesn't work . . . if the rope breaks, you let him live.'

'For goodness' sake, Graziella, don't give us the vapours now,' snapped Franz. 'What the devil do you think we're going to eat tomorrow, anyway?'

He strode into the bathroom. 'You can help me,' he threw over his shoulder at Sebastian, who had been standing quietly on the half-lit landing. 'I'll pull the plug out and pour this stuff on him. Then you bang his head on the side of the bath.'

'No,' Sebastian stepped forward into the light. 'If Miss . . . if Graziella does not wish this fish to be killed, then this fish will not be killed.'

Franz put down the bottle. A muscle twitched in his cheek. 'Why you . . . you . . . Who the blazes do you think you are, barging in here and telling me what to do?'

Considering that both men came from good families, the fight which followed was an extraordinarily dirty one. The Queensberry rules, though well-known on the Continent, might never have existed. In a sense, of course, the outcome was inevitable, for Franz was motivated only by hatred and lust for his Christmas dinner, whereas Sebastian fought for love. But, though she was almost certain of Sebastian's victory, Graziella, sprinkling chloroform on to a bath towel, was happily able to make *sure*.

Dawn broke. The bells of the Stephan's Kirche pealed out the challenge and the glory of the birth of Christ.

In the Mannhaus mansion, Graziella slept and smiled and slept again. Onkel Ernst, propped on seven goosefeather pillows, opened an eye, reflected happily that today nothing could be asked of him—no carving, no wobbling on stepladders, no candle-lighting—and closed it again.

But in the kitchen, Tante Gerda and the cook, returning from Mass, faced disgrace and ruin. Everything was ready—the chopped herbs, (bravely, the cook had agreed to mace), the wine, the cream, the lemon . . . and upstairs, swimming strongly, was the centrepiece, the *raison d'être* for days of planning and contriving, who should, for hours already, have been floating in his marinade.

As though that was not enough, as they sat down to breakfast there was a message from Franz. He was still unwell and would not be coming to dine with them. It took a full minute for the implication of this to reach Tante Gerda. When it did, she put down her head and groaned. 'Thirteen! We shall be thirteen for dinner! Oh, heavens! Gross-Tante Wilhelmina will never stand for that!'

But Fate had not finished with Tante Gerda. The breakfast dishes were scarcely cleared away when the back-door bell rang and the maid returned, struggling under a gigantic hamper.

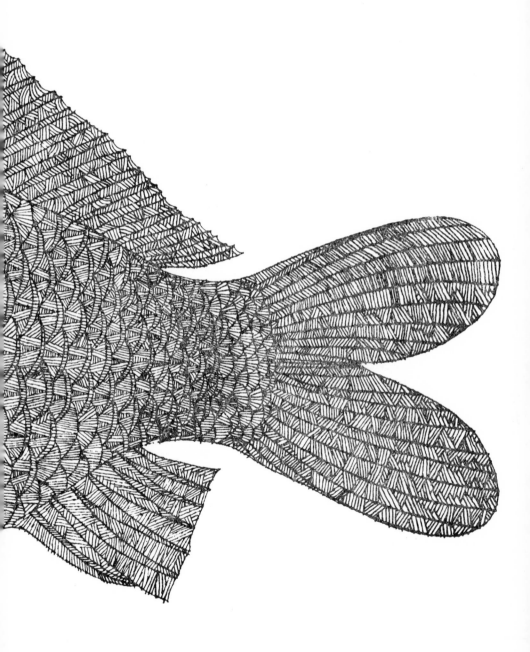

'Oh, no . . . NO!' shrieked Tante Gerda.

But it was true. Now, at the eleventh hour, with everything still to do and the shops closing fast, the Pfischingers had 'sent.'

And now it was here, the moment for which all these weeks had been the preparation. It was dusk. The little nieces boiled and bubbled in their petticoats, pursued by nursemaids with curling-tongs and ribbons. Inside 'the room', Tante Gerda, watched complacently by Onkel Ernst, climbed up and down the stepladder checking the candles, the fire bucket, the angle of the silver star. Clucking, murmuring, she ran from pile to pile of the presents spread on the vast white cloth beneath the tree. Graziella's young doctor, summoned from the laboratory, had agreed to come to dinner so that they wouldn't be thirteen. He had even somehow contrived presents for the little nieces—three tiny wooden boxes which Tante Gerda now added to their heaps.

And now all the candles were lit and she rang the sweet-toned Swiss cow-bell which was the signal that they could come in.

Though they had been huddled, straining against the door, when it was opened the little nieces came slowly, very slowly into the room, the myriad candles from the tree shining in their eyes. Behind them came Graziella, her head tilted to the glittering star and beside her the young doctor—who had given her only a single rose.

And suddenly Tante Gerda's headache lifted, and she cried a little and knew that somehow, once again, the thing she had struggled for was there. Christmas.

You'd think that was the end of the story, wouldn't you? But my mother, telling it years later, liked to go on just a bit further. To the moment when the little nieces, having politely unwrapped a mountain of costly irrelevancies, suddenly burst into shrieks of ecstasy and fulfilment. For, opening Sebastian's wooden boxes, they found, for each of them, a tiny, pink-eyed, *living* mouse.

Or further still. To the family at table—white damask, crystal goblets, crimson roses in a bowl. To the little nieces (the youngest wobbling fearfully on her pile of cushions), each pocket of each knicker-leg bulgy with a sleepy, smuggled mouse. To Onkel Ernst magnificent in his bandages, and Graziella and Sebastian glowing like comets . . . To the sudden stiffening, knuckles whitening round the heavy spoons, as Tante Gerda brought in the huge silver serving-dish.

And the sigh of released breath, the look of awed greed as she set it down. Egg-garnished, gherkin-bedecked, its translucent depths glittering with exotic fishes and tiny jewelled vegetables, the celebrated concoction quivered gently before them. Lampreys in aspic! Truly—most truly, the Pfischingers had sent.

The littlest niece,when she grew up and became my mother, liked to end the story there. But I always made her go on just a little further. To the day after Christmas. To the house of the Pfischingers on the other side of Vienna. To Herr Doktor Pfischinger, a small, bald, mild little man ascending the stairs to his bathroom. He is carrying a long-bladed knife, a sledge-hammer, a *blunderbuss.* . . .

The Chef has Imagination
or
It's too Hard to do it Easy

Hark to a lettuce lover.
I consider lettuce a blessing.
And what do I want on my lettuce?
Simply a simple dressing.

But in dining-car and hostel
I grow apoplectic and dropsical;
Is this *dressing* upon my lettuce,
Or is it a melting popsicle?

A dressing is not the meal, dears,
It requires nor cream nor egg,
Nor butter nor maple sugar,
And neither the nut nor the meg.

A dressing is not a compote,
A dressing is not a custard;
It consists of pepper and salt,
Vinegar, oil, and mustard.

It is not paprika and pickles,
Let us leave those to the Teutons;
It is not a pinkish puddle
Of grenadine and Fig Newtons.

Must I journey to France for dressing?
It isn't a baffling problem;
Just omit the molasses and yoghurt,
The wheat germ, and the Pablum.

It's oil and vinegar, dears,
No need to tiddle and toil;
Just salt and pepper and mustard,
And vinegar, and oil.

For Brillat-Savarin, then, and Hoyle,
Stick, friends, to vinegar and oil!
Yachtsman, jettison boom and spinnaker,
Bring me oil and bring me vinegar!
Play the music of Haydn or Honegger,
But lace it with honest oil and vinegar!
Choir in church or mosque or synagogue,
Sing, please, in praise of oil and vinegogue.
I'm not an expert, just a beginneger,
But I place my trust in oil and vinegar.
May they perish, as Remus was perished by Romulus,
Who monkey with this, the most sacred of formulas.

OGDEN NASH

Claret for Bach . . .

BY ROBIN ORR*

Y first lesson is always a conventional one—
no music, no practice, just a heart-to-heart
talk on the fundamentals of the art of singing.
Let us go to Thomson's Café in Sixth Avenue
and sip claret, which the Italians consider a great stimulant
to the vocal chords.'

I think it was the comedian, James T. Powers, who thus described his first singing lesson. Some singers have been devoted to
port, others to madeira. Caruso, I am told, always took a glass
of whisky. This is surprising because it is generally agreed that
spirits are bad for the vocal organs. For myself, if I had to sing
for my supper, I would take the precaution of having half a pint
of wine first.

Wine and music are excellent companions, and they have certain features in common. Neither the wine in the bottle, nor the
music when the notes have been committed to paper, is of much
account. It is necessary to take further steps; to taste and to
perform. Only then is the cycle of creation completed. But this
is not all. There is long life in certain wines, most notably madeira,
so that a man may taste with pleasure and curiosity a bottle from
a vintage first enjoyed by his father or grandfather before him.
Music takes us further, since an intelligent performance can bring
to life the notes written down centuries earlier.

Maybe there are wines appropriate to various different kinds of
music. So far as I am aware, there has been no enquiry into this
intriguing subject, but on the impulse of the moment I would
suggest claret for Bach, burgundy for Beethoven, hock with
Mendelssohn, Château d'Yquem for Richard Strauss and Pouilly
Blanc Fumé from the Château du Nozet for Stravinsky.

It may be a matter for argument whether or not wine enhances
the enjoyment of listening to music, save in solitude, since wine
stimulates conversation and this runs counter to the proper
appreciation of a symphony or string quartet. I have never yet
enjoyed a good bottle of port the more because my host insisted
on having Beethoven on the gramophone at the same time. On
the other hand, the occasional *longueurs* in the works of the
master have been greatly eased, for me at least, by a judicious

*Professor of Music, Cambridge University

use of alchohol in one form or another. This apart, it is only in the lighter ditties that the conscientious listener is likely to find time to attend to his glass. Old Merrythought, in the *Knight of the Burning Pestle* spoke with more sense than he may have realized when he called: 'Be merry, boys! some light music, and more wine.'

But the arts of St Cecilia have been an accompaniment to food and wine for many centuries. In the account of his tour of Central Europe in 1772, Dr Burney described Vienna, where 'There was music every day during dinner . . . at the inn where I lodged . . . . but it was usually bad, particularly that of a band of wind instruments, which constantly attended the ordinary . . . all so miserably out of tune that I wished them a hundred miles off.'

Today, if not in times past, the function of music during dinner is no more than to provide a background to conversation. In this respect it is much to be preferred to the dancing girls of old, whom you could not have enjoyed without taking your eyes off the table. And the modern dinner-dance is the ruination of many a good meal and of the wine which should accompany it.

Here, in our fickle climate, what would we not give to be transported through time and space to Attica for one of those ancient festivals in honour of Dionysus, complete with songs, dances and phallic processions? Since the first tasting of the new wine could occur but once a year, the seasonal nature of these festivities was a powerful stimulus; and I suspect it is not simply the prospect of a thick hill-mist or drenching rain that has prevented bacchanalia from developing around the distilleries of Speyside.

Music and wine together combine to produce a state of joyousness, particularly when they are taken in a charming setting, whether it be in a splendid hall with fine linen and silver, under the olive trees with cicadas chafing in the sun, or in a smoky tavern with a Virgilian Copa Surisca to liven it up.

We can learn a great deal about the musical instruments in use at different times by studying classical paintings and reliefs, but little about the wine save the vessels in which it was served. The enchanting painting by Giorgione, *Le Concert Champêtre*, clearly illustrates the instruments, but it is only by a process of deduction that one comes to the conclusion that the beaker in the hand of one of the young women apparently contains water. Titian's *Bacchanal* (in the Prado) clearly depicts stronger liquors, but we cannot identify them.

Dresden d. 18t 1824.

C: M: von Weber

Haydn

votre très humble et très obéissant
serviteur

Boïeldieu

Canone a 3 Voci di L: Cherubini, offerto a Madamigella Sontag. 1829

Andantino

Parti coll'ombra e ver l'ingannatrice il piacer, ma la mia tiranna di o I: dolo del cor mio coll'ombra non parti coll' ombra coll'ombra non parti. se mai se mai per un momen—to sognai d'esser feli—ce sognai d'esser feli—ce d'esser fe—li—ce s'accre—sca il mi—o tormen—to quando ri—torna il di.

se mai se mai per un momen—to sognai, sognai, s'accresca il mio tormento quando ritor—na quando ritorna il di.

Accompagnamento.

Fine

Si riprende sempre dal ritornello

Schwerin den 7t Okt.
1859

et je vous prie d'agréer, chère Madame
l'assurance de mon profond respect

(Professeur au Conservatoire Impérial de musique)

Chopin - by Delacroix

Singing and dancing were inseparable from feasting in times past. We remember *les entremets*—the in-between dishes—which acquired this name from the entertainments provided between the main courses at banquets in the fourteenth and fifteenth centuries. These consisted of dances such as the Branles sautés (which I am afraid has nothing to do with the culinary art), along with instrumental and vocal music.

Plutarch considered that music and dancing helped to prevent quarrelling amongst excited members of the company in the later stages of feasting. Similarly, an outward show of good-will in many a Tudor home may have owed something to the singing of madrigals, seated round the table after dinner, with throats suitably conditioned by plenty of sherris sack.

Roger North, in the reign of Charles II, lamented the coming of a new kind of music which, being too difficult for the amateur to play, left country families without the sober form of recreation to which they had long been accustomed: 'When wee know not how to pass the time, wee fall to drink. If company is not at home, wee goe out to marketts and meetings to find such as will joyn in debauchery, and the country is dull for want of plentifull and exquisite debauchery.'

Music still has its place at formal banquets in the City and elsewhere. When I was an organist, I was required to direct madrigals after dinner at College feasts, and the singing of a Grace anthem was the order of the day. It was not always easy to find suitable pieces; but it grieves me to report that my suggestion that we might consider Tallis's *Purge me, O God* was not taken up.

Mit vollkommener Hochachtung
ergebenst

Berlin d. 3 Januar
1844.

Felix Mendelssohn Bartholdy

. . . and Moselwein for Mozart

BY OTTO LOEB

LTHOUGH I have been forty years in the wine trade, music has always been my great hobby, and I was delighted to be introduced to John Christie, the founder of Glyndebourne, after the first season in 1934, when I came to England on a visit: I had never before heard of an opera house set in the country. John Christie, or Captain Christie as he used to be called in those days, was not an easy man to deal with. He was a great character with a definite will, never ready to make concessions: Glyndebourne reflects his strong will in every way. I soon found out that he was a wine-lover with a very outspoken taste for sweet, full-bodied wines. This was so developed that even very fine but dry wines were refused as 'rubbish'. Captain Christie in a letter published in a wine-trade paper during the war pointed out: 'One's palate depends on the food of the country, or even of the district, on the cooking, the water, the drink of the country, and a change of frontiers alters one's palate. On the south and the north side of Bideford Bay a German wine tastes quite differently. The climate is different.'

Captain Christie thought that only German wines would be right for Mozart, and as the first three seasons concentrated on Mozart's best known operas, there were only German wines on the list 'from the Glyndebourne cellars'. These lists were unique. They contained quotations about wine from the Greek classical writers for which not Mr Christie but his one time colleague at Eton, C. M. Wells, was responsible. The fullest and sweetest Palatinate wines dominated the lists, echoing their master's voice. In 1936, for instance, the only listed Rhine wines were 1933 or 1934 fairly heavy Forster or Deidesheimer spätlese and one

Beerenauslese at prices from 15s to 23s. Moselles ranged from 16s to 35s for 1934 Wehlener Sonnenuhr feinste auslese of J. J. Prüm and 1934 Scharzhofberger Beerenauslese of A. J. Koch, but no dry wines at all. Both Dr Fritz Busch, the chief conductor, and Professor Carl Ebert, the producer, were connoisseurs of wines and were regularly at Mr Christie's table during the interval. They, like some guests, were getting tired of drinking only sweet wines. Fritz Busch asked me one day: 'Can't you smuggle a bottle of dry Moselle for me to Mr Christie's table?' It was an endless, not very successful, struggle with Captain Christie to try to convince him that not everybody shared his taste for sweet wines.

It was gratifying, though, that the most famous hock in this country, 'Liebfraumilch', never found its way to Glyndebourne. Here the master and the supplier were for once unanimous in banning it. Gradually the list began to show a little more variety, and in 1937 even a dry 1935 Erdener Herrenberg was admitted, an estate-bottled Moselle at 16s. French wines were still almost entirely excluded. A single burgundy appeared, however, on the 1936 list, simply and typically announced as 'Unknown, reputed to be 1924', at 10s. This must have been a discovery from the Glyndebourne cellars. However, some concessions had to be made when a sort of anti-Nazi boycott threatened the sale of German wines from 1938 onwards. As a result, the 1939 list offered 1928 Mouton, 1928 Filhot and 1929 Yquem (24s); from Burgundy the 1929 Pommard les Grands Epenots and 1934 Bâtard Montrachet at 16s, but no wines from Alsace. The sale of German wines, which was 60 bottles in the first season, had reached more than 4,000 bottles before the war, based on a season of approximately 6 weeks or 37 nights. Glyndebourne could then still afford to offer *Beeren-* or *Trockenbeerenauslesen* which—in spite of an unusually high profit—were still no more than 50s per bottle. The 1934 Zeltinger Sonnuhr feinste Beerenauslese of J. J. Prüm was undoubtedly the finest of all pre-war wines listed. Royal visitors were always entertained in Mr Christie's house, and after a visit by Queen Elizabeth (now the Queen Mother), who had the 1934 Zeltinger with the Christies, there was some correspondence with Buckingham Palace. Mr Christie gave me a copy of a letter he wrote in January 1938 to King George VI's Financial Secretary, parts of which are here published with Mr George Christie's permission, a letter so typical of his father:

The Financial Secretary to H.M. The King,   8th January, 1938.
Buckingham Palace,
London.

Dear Sir,

I cannot read your signature, and, of course, I ought to know who is Financial Secretary. My impression is that it was Adeane, but I can see a dot over your signature, which makes this impossible. I hope that you will forgive me, but I am a long way off finding out. . . .

I can answer your enquiries categorically:

1. The wine in question is wine from the Rhein and Mosel districts, including the Saar and Ruwer districts. I bought about 1100 bottles last year.

2. I buy all there is of any individual wine. The German wines consist of separate casks which have not been filled from some lake of wine and every cask, even though it has the same name, has a different taste and a different price. . . .

5. I should be prepared to pass on any of these wines at the price which I pay. I am not a Wine Merchant and I am therefore not looking for any profit on the sale of these wines, except, of course, where they are sold in our restaurant. In that case the profit forms a subsidy to the opera.

6. These wines are drinkable now and, I believe, should be drunk within 10 years of their vintage. They vary in prices from 2-3 Marks to 15 Marks a bottle. The 2-3 Marks make pleasant drinking, the 9 Marks very good indeed and the 15 Marks are just a speciality for the Connoisseurs to smack their lips on.

7. There is practically no sale in England of good German wines. The English public buy at once if the wine is called 'Liebfraumilch', but it is apparently a trade name given to any rubbish sent over to the English market. There is a small vineyard called 'Liebfraumilch' which has little and, as a rule, nothing to do with the wine called 'Liebfraumilch' sent to England.

8. We have made a speciality of German wines for our Festival, sales of the last four years being 60 bottles, 966, 2500, and 4000.

9. The amounts which I could pass on to Their Majesties could be large or small, but they would presumably be small, in view of the fact that we have supplies available at Glyndebourne, and because it would presumably be better that they should have individual attention from me in respect of any wine which they wished to have.

10. I find that German wines do not taste equally well in all places. Glyndebourne seems to be good. Tapley is bad. It is the same problem, I suppose, as the German Cigar. It is therefore conceivable

that Balmoral or Sandringham might be unfortunate. I suppose one can only find this out by trial. Red wines are good at Tapley. It is one of those queer things.

If there is anything I can do I am, of course, at your service.

Yours sincerely,

JOHN CHRISTIE

When war broke out, there was still a considerable stock of German wines left—buried under the steep hillside where a unique wine cellar had been built by Mr Christie, who was his own architect. It was very wet, as the rain came through the roof and often damaged the labels. Some of the wines would have lived long enough to survive the war, but one can well understand that Mr Christie wanted to realise a stock of about 15,000 bottles of German wines, all estate-bottled and almost unobtainable elsewhere. The auction of 'the famous wines from the Glyndebourne cellars' took place at Restells in 1942. Every bottle was sold at prices higher even than the former restaurant prices. Mr Christie was very pleased with the result of the auction. His statement soon afterwards that, 'there will only be iced lager after the war, should Glyndebourne survive,' was never taken seriously. But the Glyndebourne cellars were absolutely empty. Mr Christie came to me a little later to beg a few bottles of wine, as he had nothing left!

When in 1946 Glyndebourne was opened again it was not on pre-war lines but in order to give the English Opera Group a chance to perform Britten's *The Rape of Lucretia* and *Albert Herring*. Wines from an outside caterer were offered at very high prices, but not on pre-war lines.

But in 1950, with the reappearance of Dr Fritz Busch and Professor Ebert, the opera was almost back to normal. The wine list was again nearly the old familiar shape—though there were no more Greek or Latin quotations. However, Mr Christie left it from now to the caterers to select the wines, or rather to accept recommendations. From a personal point of view I regretted this, as it deprived me of the amusing meetings we had had in the past. On the other hand it now became easier—and without opposition—to introduce a wine list to meet the taste of everyone. Alsatian wines made their first appearance and among the Rhine wines were two great 1945s, one a Beerenauslese from Johannisberg, and a few clarets, red burgundies, and a Bâtard

Montrachet of the Louis Poirier estate, successive vintages of which remained on the list for many years. Even English mead made a short appearance on the 1951 list, followed by 'Iced Cups', but otherwise the number of German wines in every season totalled about seven or eight Rhine wines and four or five Moselles. About 15 French wines, more red than white, would complete the list. The principle of listing estate-bottled wines was kept up almost all the time. There were always one or two wines at about 19s to avoid some criticism that the wine prices were too high, but I can confirm that the caterers very often kept their profit down and sold the wines at less than the usual margin. One could therefore find once again 1945 Deidesheimer Beerenauslese and 1937 Forster Beerenauslese at 50s and 55s a bottle, while the top prices even for older clarets did not exceed 35s. The excellent 1947 Bâtard Montrachet was offered during the seasons 1952/3 at 35s. Steinwein in Bocksbeutels was introduced in 1953 and has been popular ever since.

It was interesting to observe that Mr Christie very rarely used wines from the wine list when entertaining on his own table. He had in fact acquired a sort of obsession that wine prices altogether were too high and that it was a waste to spend more than 7s or 8s for a bottle of wine. Therefore on some occasions guests were rather disappointed to find on his table the cheapest possible Sauternes—or even barley-water—which he would have described as 'rubbish' in his earlier days.

Sales are now steady, from season to season, and German wines acount for 55 per cent of the total. The French red wines sell best on the cooler evenings of May and early June.

Over the years I have come to recognise a link between the particular opera being performed and the wines the public chose. If it happend to be a serious dramatic opera such as *Alceste* by Gluck or *Idomeneo* by Mozart, there was altogether less drinking but more demand for the drier wines. But a sparkling performance of Richard Strauss's *Der Rosenkavalier* or Rossini's *Barber of Seville* resulted in more sales of champagne or elegant Rhine wines. In *La Cenerentola* by Rossini a wine-tasting takes place on the stage—and the audience drinks more wine. During Bank Holiday week there is usually a visible change in the audience and the result is considerably lower wine sales. On the other hand, it became evident that the cheapest wines on the Glyndebourne list are, as so often, not the best sellers. One must not overlook the fact that most people have already paid in advance at least part of the considerable expenses connected with a visit to the opera—a psychological factor which encouraged Mr Christie in pre-war days to charge as much as possible for the wines.

It is good to look back over thirty years of supplying wine to Glyndebourne and realise that it is possible in this country to offer and sell on a famous wine list tens of thousands of bottles of selected German wines—and not one bottle of Liebfraumilch!

Glyndebourne Festival Opera House

Wines from the Glyndebourne Cellars

πῖνε γέρον καὶ ζῆθι. (AGATHIAS.)

∷ ∷ ∷

μηκέτι ὑδροπότει ἀλλ' οἴνῳ ὀλίγῳ χρῶ διὰ τὸν στομαχόν σου. (ST. PAUL.)

∷ ∷ ∷

οὐκ ἔστιν ἄλλος οἶνος ἡδίων πιεῖν. (CLEARCHUS.)

∷ ∷ ∷

οἶνον τοι, Μενέλαε, θεοὶ ποίησαν ἄριστον
θνητοῖς ἀνθρώποισιν ἀποσκεδάσαι μελεδώνας. (CYPRION.)

∷ ∷ ∷

ἀνδρί γε κεκμηῶτι μένος μέγα οἶνος ἀέξει. (HOMER.)

The cover of the 1936 wine list

159

MOSEL, SAAR, RUWER WINES

			PRICE ½-BOTTLE	BOTTLE

1. 1934 Zeltinger Sonnuhr, Feinste Beerenauslese, Original Abfüllung
   Joh. Jos. Prüm ... ...   —   50/-

   πῖνε γέρον καὶ ζῆθι. (AGATHIAS.)

2. 1934 Kaseler Dominikanerberg, Feinste Trockenbeerenauslese,
   Original Abfüllung, Burghard v. Nell ... ...   —   45/-

   οἰνόν τοι, Μενέλαε, θεοὶ ποίησαν ἄριστον
   θνητοῖς ἀνθρώποισιν ἀποσκεδάσαι μελεδώνας. (Cypria.)

3. 1934 Wehlener Sonnenuhr Feinste Auslese Weingut Pruem ...   17/-   30/-

   τὸν τὰς ὀφθῦς αἴροντα συμπείθεις γελᾶν. (DIPHILUS.)

4. 1934 Scharzhofberger Beerenauslese, Wachstum von Apollinar
   Joseph Koch, Original-Kellerabzug 17/-   30/-

   χρύσω χρυσοτέρα. (SAPPHO.)
   φάρμακον ἄριστον οἶνος. (ALCAEUS.)

5. 1935 Erdener Herrenberg, Original Abfüllung, Weingut Rich,
   Jos. Berres ... ...   —   16/-

   ὁ παλαιὸς οἶνος οὐ πρὸς ἡδονὴν μόνον ἀλλὰ καὶ πρὸς ὑγίειαν
   προσφορώτερος. (ATHENAEUS.)

RHEIN WINES FROM THE RHEINPFALZ AND RHEINGAU

7. 1933 Forster Kirchenstück Riesling, Spätlese, Weingut Dr. Deinhard
   Deidesheim ... ...   —   23/-

   ἀλλὰ τόδ' ἀμβροσίης καὶ νέκταρος ἐστὶν ἀπορρώξ. (HOMER.)

8. 1934 Forster Jesuitengarten Riesling, Spätlese, Original Abfüllung,
   J. L. Wolf Erben 11/-   20/-

   ὄζει ἴων, ὄζει δὲ ῥόδων, ὄζει δ' ὑακίνθου. (HOMER.)

9. 1934 Forster Langenacker Riesling Auslese, Original Abfüllung,
   Reichsrat von Buhl 10/-   19/-

   ἡδὺν ἀκηράσιον θεῖον ποτόν. (HOMER.)

10. 1933 Deidesheimer Rennpfad Riesling, Weingut Reichsrat von Buhl,
    Original Abfüllung ... ... 11/-   —

    ἀμβροσία καὶ νέκταρ ὁμοῦ. (HOMER.)

Pages 2 and 3 of the 1937 wine list

				PRICE
			½-BOTTLE	BOTTLE

11. 1934 Deidesheimer Kieselberg Riesling, Weingut Bassermann-Jordan   —   **15/-**

οὐδεὶς φιλοπότης ἐστὶν ἄνθρωπος κακός. (ALEXIS.)

12. 1933 Winkeler Hasensprung Riesling, Wachstum Jakob Sterzel
(Rheingau) ... ...   —   **10/6**

ὅταν πίω τοῦτ', εὐθὺς ὑγιὴς γίγνομαι. (EPILYCUS.)

HUNGARIAN WINES

13. 1932 Olasz Rizling, A Magyar Kegyestanitòrend Dörgicsei
Gazdasàgànak Termése ... ...   —   **10/-**

14. 1929 Somlai Kéknyelü, Bàrò Malcomes Albert Termèse ... ...   —   **10/-**

CHAMPAGNES

21. 1919 Veuve Cliquot Dry England ... ...   —   **30/-**

ὑπερφυῶς ὡς τὴν χήραν φιλῶ. (Who?)

22. 1928 Binet United Kingdom Cuvée **10/-**   **20/-**

οἶνον λευκῷ πεπυκασμένον ἄνθει. (ARCHESTRATUS.)

BURGUNDY

31. 1932 Nuits St. Georges (Colcombret Frères) ... ...   —   **10/-**

31A. 1915 Romanée ... ... **10/-**   —

CLARET

31B. 1923 Gruaud Larose, Grand Vin, Mis en bouteilles au chateau
Faure Bethmann Propriétaire ... ...   —   **15/-**

WHITE BORDEAUX

32. 1913 Sigalas Rabaud, Premier Cru Classé ... ...   —   **25/-**

ἀνδρί γε κεκμηῶτι μένος μέγα οἶνος ἀέξει. (HOMER.)

				PRICE	
				½-BOTTLE	BOTTLE

M 1. 1934 Zeltinger Sonnuhr Feinste Beerenauslese Original Abfüllung
J. J. Prüm (Best cask of the vintage) ... ... — 50/-

πίνε γέρον καὶ ζῆθι. (AGATHIAS.)

R 2. 1934 Kaseler Dominikanerberg Feinste Trockenbeerenauslese
Original Abfüllung Burghard v. Nell ... ... — 40/-

οἶνόν τοι, Μενέλαε, θεοὶ ποίησαν ἄριστον
θνητοῖς ἀνθρώποισιν ἀποσκεδάσαι μελεδώνας. (Cypria.)

S 3. 1934 Scharzhöfberger Beerenauslese Original Abfüllung Apollinar
Joseph Koch 17/- 35/-

χρύσω χρυσοτέρα. (SAPPHO.)
φάρμακον ἄριστον οἶνος. (ALCAEUS.)

M 4. 1934 Wehlener Sonnenuhr Feinste Auslese Original Abfüllung
Weingut J. J. Prüm 17/- 30/-

τὸν τὰς ὀφθῦς αἴροντα συμπείθεις γελᾶν. (DIPHILUS.)

S 5. 1935 Ayler Herrenberger Feinste Auslese Original Abfüllung
Bischöfl Konvikt ... ... — 26/-

ἀνδρί γε κεκμηῶτι μένος μέγα οἶνος ἀέξει. (HOMER.)

M 6. 1935 Erdener Herrenberg Original Abfüllung Rich Jos. Berres ... — 16/-

ὁ παλαιὸς οἶνος οὐ πρὸς ἡδονὴν μόνον ἀλλὰ καὶ πρὸς ὑγίειαν
προσφορώτερος. (ATHENAEUS.)

RHEIN WINES FROM THE RHEINPFALZ AND RHEINHESSEN

P 7. 1936 Deidesheimer Martenweg Riesling Original Abfüllung Reichsrat
von Buhl 6/- 10/-

P 8. 1935 Deidesheimer Grain Riesling Original Abfüllung Geh. Rat. Dr.
von Bassermann-Jordan ... ... — 16/-

οὐκ ἔστιν ἄλλος οἶνος ἡδίων πιεῖν (CLEARCHUS.)

P 9. 1934 Forster Jesuitengarten Riesling Spätlese Original Abfüllung
J. L. Wolf Erben 11/- 20/-

ὄζει ἴων, ὄζει δὲ ῥόδων, ὄζει δ' ὑακίνθου. (HOMER.)

P 10. 1936 Forster Fleckinger Riesling Wachstum Weingut Weber.
This cask was bottled in England under the personal supervision
of Glyndebourne ... ... — 12/-

ὅταν πίω τοῦτ', εὐθὺς ὑγιὴς γίγνομαι. (EPILYCUS.)

M = Mosel   S = Saar   R = Ruwer   P = Palatinate

Pages 2 and 3 of the 1938 wine list

RHEIN WINES FROM THE RHEINPFALZ AND RHEINHESSEN (CONTINUED)

			PRICE ½-BOTTLE	BOTTLE

P 11. 1934 Deidesheimer Kieselberg Riesling Auslese Original Abfüllung Reichsrat von Buhl **15/–** **28/–**

ἡδὺν ἀκηράσιον θεῖον ποτόν. (HOMER.)

P 12. 1935 Forster Jesuitengarten Riesling Beerenauslese Original Abfüllung W. Spindler ... ... — **40/–**

ἀλλὰ τόδ' ἀμβροσίης καὶ νέκταρός ἐστιν ἀπορρώξ. (HOMER.)

RG 13A. 1934 Hochheimer Reichestal Gutsverwaltung der Stadt Frankfurt — **11/–**

14A. 1932 Deidesheimer Schloss Gewürztraminer Original Abfüllung Geh. Rat. Dr. von Bassermann-Jordan ... ... — **14/–**

CHAMPAGNES

21. 1928 Veuve Cliquot Dry England **15/–** **30/–**

ὑπερφυῶς ὡς τὴν χήραν φιλῶ. (Who?)

22. 1928 Binet United Kingdom Cuvée **10/–** **20/–**

οἶνον λευκῷ πεπυκασμένον ἄνθει. (ARCHESTRATUS.)

BURGUNDY

31A. 1923 Chambertin ... ... — **14/–**

CLARET

31B. 1925 Château Cheval Blanc ... ... — **12/–**

HAUT BARSAC

32. 1924 Chateau Climens ... ... — **13/–**

P = Palatinate   RG = Rheingau

Pink Champagne

BY JAMES LAVER

HEN I was a boy in Liverpool, more than half a century ago, I was making my way, on a half-holiday, to the public library. In a wine shop near the Adelphi Hotel (and why I should be looking in a wine shop I don't know, for my family was strictly T.T.) my attention was suddenly drawn to a show-card in the window. It depicted an old gentleman (old! I suppose he was about fifty) and a young lady showing what was for the period a rather daring amount of black-stockinged leg. She was also extremely décolleté. Both of them were holding up glasses of a rather peculiar shape filled with a liquid which seemed to be slightly pink. The slogan read: 'Wild Oats. A Late Sowing.' This, I am afraid, conveyed nothing to me at all, and even the word 'Champagne' in a corner of the card was remote from my experience. It is surprising perhaps that I should have remembered the advertisement at all, and whether Mumm or Heidsieck, or Pol Roger had paid for it I shall now never know.

Later in life, however, I met the old gentleman, or someone extremely like him. I think of him as the typical Edwardian uncle. Most families have, or have had, such a personage who wore a flower in his coat, a carefully tended moustache, now white, and probably an eye-glass. And whatever we, or our parents, may have thought of Uncle George, this much at least seemed certain, that he had a very good time. In retrospect, we can see that his perpetual euphoria had two causes; first a sense of security—there seemed no reason why his world should not go on for ever—and second the probability that he was always just a little bit under the influence of alcohol. Why not indeed, when champagne could be purchased in the long bar of the Cri at 6d. a glass? The champagne was probably pink, like so many other things at that time, *The Pink 'Un* for example, and the discreet powder on ladies' cheeks, and indeed there is no reason, except modern snootiness, why good champagne should not be pink. It is only a matter of leaving the must a little longer on the skins of the black grapes (champagne comes from about 70% black grapes and only 30% white). Certainly, Edward VII liked it pink and he liked it decanted in a jug, so that he could 'help himself'.

In retrospect, the Edwardian age is already beginning to detach itself from history to become one of those little islands in Time on which (and in which) the imagination loves to dwell. There are several such islands floating about in the mind and they have this in common: they are the scene of a perpetual fête. There is a party going on, although we—alas!—are born too late to have our share in it.

Such a party was the Edwardian period, before people had become too serious to enjoy themselves, when bridge and bicycles were still fascinating novelties, when income tax was a flea-bite and the British pound was received with respect in the remotest corners of the globe, a party presided over by the portly and cheerful figure of the Monarch himself, who was so clearly enjoying himself, and expecting his subjects to enjoy themselves also.

The Edwardian age was probably the last period in history when the fortunate thought they could give pleasure to others by displaying their good fortune before them. All most reprehensible, no doubt, in our egalitarian eyes, and yet I am by no means convinced that the general level of happiness was not higher, even among the 'down-trodden masses', than it is today. At least success meant something; there was something to succeed *into*, and a novel which sold 50,000 copies or a play that ran for five hundred nights gave you a villa at Le Touquet or a yacht at Cannes.

Writers and fashionable painters had probably the best time they have ever had in the history of the world. The days when they had been sent to dine in the servants' hall were long over, the days when they lived in remote country cottages and wondered ruefully who was going to buy their work, had not yet arrived. They were admitted to the party and, if they had arrived a little late, they made up for it by helping themselves lavishly to the champagne and caviar.

The Edwardian world was dominated by the idea of the Season. It was indeed almost the only rule, this regulation by the period of the year. You could do almost anything so long as you did it at the right time. In May, June and July, you had to be in London and were expected to show yourselves in the proper places: in Bond Street at eleven o'clock in the morning or in the Row for Church Parade. The motor-car was an amusing toy; it had not yet driven the carriages away from Hyde Park. And, of course, the bold spirits who 'went in' for motoring needed a special outfit to enable them to withstand the penetrating dust and the terrifying speed of these new mechanical wonders. When the Season was over one fled to the moors; to be seen in London in August was an unforgivable lapse in social virtue. And when winter came there was always Monte.

The whole of the Riviera was then considered entirely as a winter resort; it had not occurred to any fashionable being to go there in the summer, for sun-bathing had not been invented, and gloves and parasols protected even hands and faces from the least suspicion of tan. One left Victoria for Cannes or Cap Martin secure in the knowledge that, apart from the quaint inhabitants, one would not meet anyone who was not, more or less, of one's own social class. Of course there was always a sprinkling of foreign adventurers (or what would Mr Phillips Oppenheim have found to write about?) but one could always guard one's daughters from their clutches and give oneself the pleasure of snubbing them in the Casino.

Home again, one paid a round of visits to 'luxurious hunting-lodges' in the Midlands, where, after a brisk day with the Quorn or the Cottesmore one could indulge in the dangerous delights of bridge, or the even more dangerous delights of flirtation. Dangerous because, although duelling was long over in England, the social world still frowned upon divorce. The mere whisper of the word *divorcée* and the world of friendly faces was transformed into a vista of cold shoulders.

None-the-less, 'Society' was visibly breaking up. Perhaps that is the peculiar charm of the Edwardian epoch. The *chic* was advancing triumphantly upon the bastions of the *comme il faut*; the 'gorgeous fringes' (symbolised by the tucks and flounces of the glacé petticoat) were visibly swallowing the gown. The prestige of the successful actress has never been higher and Maudi Darrell, Pauline Chase and Gertie Millar were received as Queens (or at least as Duchesses) in their own right. Sometimes they actually *became* Duchesses.

And what splendid women they were and how gorgeously apparelled! If the Edwardian ladies could return today they would certainly consider that the modern woman had forgotten how to dress. A certain *gamine* attraction, a boyish grace, they might admit, but Elegance—no! For those were the days of elaborate *toilettes* with frills sweeping to the ground, petticoats de luxe, the apotheosis of *frou-frou*. The waists were tiny and the peculiar invention of the strangely named 'Health Corset' gave the figure that curious S-shape, so typical of the time. The late Philip Guedalla once described a noble survivor of that spacious epoch as 'figure-head of no mean ship'. The ample hips were thrust backward and the generous bosom forward, giving the fine lady a charming air of gracious condescension, as of one perpetually about to shake hands with the Lower Classes.

The Garden Party was the typical fête of the period, for the climate seems to have been better then than it is today, and the dresses of the day seemed almost all designed to be seen against a background of velvet lawns and noble trees, with of course in the middle distance the grey walls of one of the Stately Homes of England. When the lady tired of this she retired to her boudoir and put on something more comfortable, a tea-gown perhaps, 'adhering' in the charming language of a contemporary advertisement, 'to no special characteristics except emphatic floppiness and looseness.' But even tea-gowns were taken seriously, as witness the words of a fashion journalist of 1906: 'A tea-gown with just pretentions to sublimity was concocted of ivory panne, narrow borderings of brown marmot and clouds of delicate lace, quaint little graduated bows of pink taffeta from chin to toe-tip forming, with the pink satin shoes, its sole note of *nuance*, if you like, of colour.' Pink again! Or was it merely that the whole world was seen through rose-coloured spectacles—or a glass of pink champagne?

Of course, it was not all sunshine in the Edwardian epoch. There were subterranean tremors and, every now and then, the rumblings on the horizon of the distant coming storm; but at least the surface pattern was gay enough. Even that makes us look backward with a certain wistfulness to an age when people were not afraid to enjoy themselves—before envy had darkened the world.

The party really came to an end with the First World War. The gambols of the Bright Young Things of the 'twenties were little more than the antics of urchins scrambling among the over-turned tables for the remains of the feast. Elegance had gone, security had gone; gaiety was no longer an exuberance, but a defence-mechanism against despair. For a world surely came to an end in 1914, and the angel with the flaming sword had shut the gates of Paradise for ever. For now the party is *quite* over, the guests are fled, indeed the house itself is being demolished or else has been taken over as a hostel for the London School of Economics.

A truce to repining! Let us, like the pilgrims of a former age, take ship for Cythera. It is a short journey we have to travel, no more than sixty years—less than the life of a man—a short journey, and yet beyond the edge of the world, for in *our* world there are no countries of escape, no Fortunate Islands, no Eldorado, no Earthly Paradise, no Kingdom East of the Sun and West of the Moon. All we can do is to compose as best we can our

Ode on a Distant Prospect of the Edwardian Epoch

Ye distant times, ye vanished hours.
Thrice happy first decade,
Above whose ghostly people towers
Great Edward's genial shade;
You used to frolic while 'twas May,
We, who have lost that generous way,
And in a meaner epoch set,
Look backward from our vale of tears,
May see, across the gulf of years,
Your glory gleaming yet.

Say, Father Time, for thou hast seen
Full many a year since then,
May not the splendour that has been
Come back to us again?
Where are they now who, long ago,
Galloped triumphant in the Row
Or drove to Epsom four-in-hand?
Or, when the Danube still was blue,
Cut ice at Prince's two, by two,
To a Hungarian band?

They rated loveliness so high,
They stood on chairs to view
The Jersey Lily driving by
And Lady Dudley too;
And she, by some esteemed the best,
Whom mortals called Cornwallis-West.
Their fame was borne by every breeze,
And gentlemen who dined alone
Would drain a bumper on their own
To one—or all—of these!

Once more, methought, I saw them stand
('Twas but a dream, I know),
That elegant and noble band
Of sixty years ago,
The men, frock-coated, tall and proud,
The women in a silken cloud,
While in the midst of them appeared
(A vision that I still retain)
The Monarch sipping pink champagne,
And smiling through his beard.

Ah, pleasant and primeval ways!
Ah, times beloved in vain!
Ah, good King Edward's golden days!
They'll never come again.
See, see how all around us wait
The Ministers of Human Fate!
Ah, if there is a man alive
Who sixty years ago foreknew
What all the world was coming to,
'Twas folly to survive.

Fruits de Mer

INKLES and whelks, cockles and oysters, spider crabs, scallops, shrimps, langoustines, mussels, prawns, the little clams known in France as *palourdes*, and in Italy as *vongole*, the big ridged heart-shaped *venus verrucosa*, called by the French *praires* and by the Italians *tartufi di mare*—sea truffles—make the open-air market stalls of the Loire estuary port of Nantes a fishy paradise, smelling of iodine, salty, dripping with seaweed and ice.

Of all these small sea-creatures displayed for sale, it is the mussels which interest me most. They are so small that hereabouts a restaurant portion of *moules marinière* must contain seven or eight dozen of the little things. Their shells are so fine they are almost transparent. The mussels themselves are quite unimaginably sweet and fresh. At the restaurant La Sirène in Nantes, an establishment where the cooking is excellently sound and imaginative, the prices extremely reasonable, I had an exquisite dish of these little mussels. They are, the proprietress told me, mussels cultivated on those posts called *bouchots* and come from Penesten, on the Morbihan coast of Brittany. They were cooked in their own liquid until they opened; fresh cream was poured over them; they were sprinkled with chopped fresh tarragon; and brought to table piled up in a tureen. Nothing could be simpler; and to us, living so few short miles across the North

Sea, not humming birds could appear more magical, nor mandrake root more unlikely.

Mussels we have in plenty, cheap and large. What they make up for in size they tend to lack in flavour and charm. From Holland, Ireland, Wales, Scotland, and from the west coast, our mussels come to London, but the little sweet ones are all left behind in the mussel-beds. If they appeared on the fishmongers' stalls nobody would want them. Few would believe they were as good as the big ones. Fewer still would want to go to the trouble of cleaning them. Which is shortsighted, because they are cleaner in the first place and easier to deal with than the monsters covered with barnacles and grit which need such endless scrubbing and rinsing, so much so that one wonders if most of the flavour is not washed out of them, a good deal of the grit still remaining. About this point, the late Henri Pellaprat, teaching chef at the Cordon Bleu School in Paris, has an interesting theory. In *Le Poisson dans la Cuisine Française* (Flammarion, 1954), he writes that most people go about the cleaning of mussels in a way calculated to put sand into them rather than to eliminate it; instead, he says, of first scraping them, one should begin by rinsing them in a quantity of cold water, turning them over and over and whirling them around. One by one you then take them out of the water and put them in a colander. Half of them will be clean already; those that are not must be scraped; as each is done, put it in a bowl, but, and this is the crux of the matter, *without water*. Only when all are cleaned should water be run over the mussels; they should then be kept on the move, the water being changed continually until it is perfectly clear. The explanation given by Pellaprat for this routine is that, put into still water all at once, the mussels start opening; when they close up again they have imprisoned within their shells the sand already in suspension in the water. In other words, explains M. Pellaprat, the more you keep the mussels moving, the more frightened they are; and the less inclination they will have to open. Ah well, possibly. It is worth paying attention to this theory, but it does mean that the mussels must be prepared only immediately before cooking, which is certainly desirable, but not always practical.

When it is a question of making the best of what we can get, a dish I had last autumn in a Paris restaurant would be well adapted to London mussels. Medium-sized cooked mussels, on the half-shell (it is of the utmost importance not to over-cook them in the first instance), were spread with a garlic and shallot butter, made in much the same way as for snails or for the Breton *palourdes farcies* which also, like snails, are sold on the Nantes fish stalls ready stuffed for cooking. Arranged on snail dishes, the mussels and their butter stuffing are protected by a layer of breadcrumbs, an addition of fresh, unthickened cream and a sprinkling of coarsely grated Gruyère. Quickly cooked in a hot oven, this is a sizzling, bubbling, richly flavoured dish; real country cooking.

The restaurant where I came across this dish was called Chez Maria in the rue du Maine. The proprietress is half-Norman, half-Breton; very likely she is the cousin or the sister-in-law of the lady in charge of the left-luggage office at the Gare Montparnasse who had directed me to the little restaurant; perhaps, arriving by train from her native shores, she never travelled much farther than the station.

There are many such people running just such restaurants or cafés in Paris. Anyone who wants to eat French regional specialities in the capital without paying the high prices of the fashionable Burgundian, Provençal, Auvergnat, Breton, Alsatian or Savoyard restaurants (in which three out of every five people eating are going to write the place up for a guide book or are begging recipes from the understandably blasé owners) could do worse than search round about, or enquire at, the main-line stations serving these provinces. There is always a sprinkling of small places owned by people like Maria; they can afford to provide their clients with a few genuine regional products at reasonable prices because they receive them direct by rail—by-passing the markets, the whole-salers, the double transport bills—from relations who are growers, poultry breeders, *charcutiers*, wine producers, fish-dealers (Maria had spanking fresh sardines the day I was there, served grilled and with a half-kilo of Breton butter on the table). The cooking in these places, although on the rough side and limited in choice, is likely to have a more authentically country flavour than that in the well-known bistros and restaurants where the proprietor has sophisticated his recipes to suit chic Parisian taste.

By this I do not mean that these re-created dishes are necessarily any the worse; they are just more evolved, less innocent. Take, for example, another mussel dish, this one from an elegant, typically Parisian and rather expensive establishment called the Berlioz, in the rue Pergolèse, not a specifically regional restaurant, but one in which a number of provincial dishes are cooked—and well-cooked. Here I ordered, from the menu, *moules marinière*. When they came, the mussels were those same delicious little Breton creatures, a great tureen of them. The sauce was yellow, just barely thickened, very light and subtle. It was, the patron told me, the result of mixing the mussel liquid with *sauce hollandaise*. It was delicious. It was perfection. What it was not was the primitive *moules marinière* known in every seaport café and to every housewife around the entire coastline of France.

At Mama's Place

BY PETER DUVAL SMITH

RIVING into Addis Ababa at night from the wild country outside, the first thing you see is a red glow reflected on the clouds that hang above the city, rather as if the place was burning down. I was reminded of the East End in the blitz, but in fact this is the red-light district, the biggest in the world and the nicest of the ones I know. Here in hundreds of tiny bar-brothels where the light-bulbs are always painted red, as if in a caricature after Maupassant, hefty glossy-black-haired Ethiopian girls in peasant costume are pouring the national drinks of *talla* and *tej*. Now *talla* is nothing much, a dark brown coarse drink made from maize that reminds you of the sort of under-nourished porter that's sold in the West of Ireland, so weak sometimes that you can see the bottom of the glass; but *tej* at its best is a drink to dream of, a dry, amber-coloured sweetish brew made from honey. It is decanted by these splendid girls from big tin kettles into little flasks shaped like altar lamps or small Chianti bottles. You drink straight from the flasks, and they cost the Ethiopian equivalent of a penny.

In Mama's place the *tej* is never at its best, because it is made of orange juice fermented with sugar; not the worst of drinks with Ethiopian mountain oranges; but not to be thought of with Imperial *tej*, which I have drunk with my friend Solomon. The very finest Imperial *tej* must be something like the mead that inspired Falstaff; in Ethiopia it is to be got only at the Emperor's table and a few others. It is made from honey collected from hollowed logs of cedar-wood hung up on the branches of eucalyptus trees. The bees make combs there, and then an Imperial serf comes and builds a fire under the tree to drive the bees away, cuts down the hanging log, and the honey is fermented into the finest *tej*. My friend Solomon is a prince of fairly high blood, and he had access to this noble drink. In the high, cold climate of Addis the sweetness is acceptable; after a few glasses the colour seems medieval gold rather than amber, and the advantage of

Imperial *tej* is a sparkling quality, such as the French call *pétillant*.

If we went out to the bars, however—and we did so nearly every night—we didn't drink at this level. Orange *tej* was good enough, tasting—to be truthful—rather like orange-juice with bitters, but stronger than you think. Before long you are doing the Twist on a bumpy mud floor with an Abyssinian maid dressed in country costume as old as the Queen of Sheba. At the end of the room is a shaky bar, with shelves behind of bottles with imitation foreign drinks, and behind that a curtain, behind which lies you can guess what.

Such a bar was Mama's place. Solomon and I used to do a tour of the bars, mostly different ones every night because there are hundreds in Addis, but we always began at Mama Tafessa's, because Solomon has a passion for girls who are tattooed. All Mama's girls are from the country, they come into Addis because that's the only place where there is plenty of work of the kind they understand, and some are from remote and savage regions of Ethiopia where the complexions are an anthropologist's day-dream. As we sat in Mama's smelly heaven, in the crimson gloom under the lacquered light bulbs, cupping our little religious flasks of amber wine, Solomon would play at spotting the tribes.

'She's from Tigre,' he'd say, pointing to a girl with a bluish barbed-wire tattoo across the bridge of her nose. 'Those people steal. And that's a Gambela girl, with the crocodile-teeth markings round her mouth. They make good wives.' Solomon's favourite was a girl from some obscure tribe on the Sudan border who had a bicycle chain motif running from ear to ear along the jawbone. When she was amused, she gave the impression of smiling with two mouths at the same time.

'Mama says she is very passionate,' he said. Mama herself was a huge, dirty woman from Harar with a tattoo on her forehead exactly like that cabalistic sign on the covers of Somerset Maugham's books that is supposed to show what a lucky life he has had. I don't know if Mama ever had any luck, but I mentioned the great man one night and she hadn't heard of him. All the same, the cultural level of Mama's place was high. There is no bar in Addis without its magazine-cover coloured portrait of Princess Margaret and her consort, but at Mama's place it is in a gilt frame. Other bars made do with the radio, tuned in permanently to the Voice of America, and dancing goes on indifferently whether it is music or propaganda. Mama scorns the radio, and has an L P and a pile of Twist discs. As an additional sign of culture, she always wears European clothes; a tubular tweed skirt and a grubby satin blouse fastened with a brooch. Mama is elaborately polite, and especially to Solomon, because of his being a prince.

Princes are fairly thick on the ground in Ethiopia, but Solomon gives good value. To look at he is like one of those little drawings in old dictionaries, illustrating a word: the picture of a Prince, nose imperious as a scimitar; flaring nostrils, always just about to twitch with arrogance; supercilious thin smile. To meet for the first time, Solomon is a bit disconcerting. You don't have the feeling you are being well thought of. You must be prepared to play second fiddle. Like all Ethiopians, Solomon has a notably low opinion of all non-Ethiopians. 'The chief characteristic of these people,' wrote the Scots traveller Bruce, who had a miserable time, 'is their self-satisfaction.' That was in the eighteenth century, but they are still pretty pleased with themselves. Solomon likes me well enough, but he cannot understand why I am not an Ethiopian. When drunk, as he often is, he believes that I am one, and he gossips about the problems of our family and what we are going to do about them, in Amharic, which I don't know.

Solomon was always polite with my endless tourist's questions, but he rarely asked any in return. He had been to England, but all he remembered of the experience was watching Stanley Matthews on television in his South Kensington hotel, and drinking unadulterated Scotch whisky for the first time. In Addis this noble, international drink costs about ten shillings a shot even in the poisoned form they serve there. Solomon's eyes would mist over as he spoke about those evenings in the Queen's Elm or the Anglesey, out of shyness speaking to no one, but swallowing a large Scotch every ten minutes at four shillings a time. Nothing else about England had impressed him. Like a good Ethiopian, he was not interested in what went on in other, inferior places. Mama, on the other hand, was hungry for foreign intelligence. Did I know, how was Sophia Loren? Was she really a bigamist? How was the Queen, by the way? Were there any new wars in the world? She would draw her elephant's foot stool closer. Tell me, she said, this thing of changing a man into a woman, what *exactly* do they do? Solomon disapproved of Mama's cosmopolitan curiosity. To him these were non-Ethiopian matters and so of no interest. If Mama went on too long with her questions, Solomon would beckon to the bicycle-chain girl and she'd come across and sit beside him. With a loving finger he would trace her wonderful tattoo. A few minutes would pass, perhaps she'd fetch another flask of *tej*.—never for herself, always for him— and then they'd slip away behind the curtain at the back of the bar, and their evening would proceed, not particularly quietly.

Mama would be pushing round the *tej* kettle, and now I could get a look at the other customers. Mostly they were students stoking up for the Twist. The Ethiopians are rather like what C. E. Montague once said of the English: permanently half-a-dozen whiskies below par. *Tej* is less strong than whisky, it is more the strength of sherry, but slowly the leeway was made up. In the meantime a tremendous silence reigned. Solomon (back from behind the curtain) stared arrogantly at the opposite wall, the students stared at the floor, the girls around the bar whispered and giggled. The *tej* flasks were filled and emptied, until eventually break-through was reached and Mama went over to the record-player and brought Chubby Checker out of his sleeve. Soon everybody was twisting, the empty *tej* kettles were bouncing on the bar, and the music was bringing people in from the street. The C. E. Montague barrier had been crashed, and now it was possible to speak to strangers without being introduced. As everywhere in the world, this laid one open to bores. One of Mama's cultural amenities was the high-class seating in her place. She had bought up some chairs from a bankrupt cinema: they were the old style with tip-up seats, joined indivisibly in pairs with a common armrest. You had to be careful whom you had sitting next to you. Once a man was settled in the tandem, he was there for the night.

Of all the bores, the worst were the language bores, those single-minded self-improvers for a free English lesson. Insanely, one evening, seeing a shy young man with a book (an Ethiopian intellectual!), I asked him over for a penn'orth of *tej*.

'What are you reading?' He handed me the book. It was *'Oliver Twist* by Charles Dickens, abridged by J. C. MacPhail, author of *David Copperfield, Henry IV, Part II, Pride and Prejudice,* etc., etc.' J. C. MacPhail had reduced *Oliver Twist* to eighty pages. On page one the young man had underlined the difficult words, pending translation by some helpful English speaker. I saw they were words like *porridge*. I gave the book back in a flash.

'Why do you want to learn English?' I said.

'Sir, I wish to be a business man.'

In the next tandem Solomon pulled a face. Business is a sore point with the Ethiopian nobility. Traditionally they are feudal landowners who do not stoop to commerce, but the wind of change has blown unkindly, and these days Solomon is forced to work as an airline clerk.

'Why do you want to be a business man?' I asked.

'Because business is the cause of civilization, sir.'

'What!' said Solomon.

'Business men have made every great nation.' The young man turned to Solomon.

'Admit to me, sir, there are no business men among monkeys. That is why they remain monkeys. They are nothing but chatterers. Do not be a chatterer, sir. Nothing can be done by talk.'

In another age Solomon would have had his head on the end of a spear. Instead he stood stiffly, and his old cinema seat flipped up with a bang. He threw a goodnight to Mama, nodded imperiously to me, and strode to the door. This grand exit was rather spoiled by the bumps in the trodden mud floor, which made him trip, and the fact that the door, which anyway was a sack on a hook, was blocked by an old man dressed in a filthy toga-like robe supporting himself, like a Biblical character, on a rough-hewn stick. While Solomon waited, furiously, I said goodnight to the young man. He was gazing at the picture of Lord Snowdon.

'Tell me,' he said, 'Is he a good king?'

This wasn't the exit line, because Mama the peacemaker rushed across with two thimble-sized glasses of *makra*. This is an oily distillate of grain, so-called colourless but in fact having a grim, bluish tinge. It is reputed to be able to remove nail polish and cure warts. It is the kind of horrible exotic drink (like Chinese Mao Tai or Cyprus double-distilled brandy) that causes a premonitory headache the moment it hits the bottom of your stomach. It is, of course, a war- rather than a peace-making drink, and Solomon was still sober enough to refuse. I put mine back, thanked Mama, and off we went, through the sacking into the dark lane outside.

Between the *tej* houses we stumbled along the rutted lanes, the wild medieval figures of present-day Ethiopia lurching by us. From each of the little red houses came the sounds of music and laughter. Wherever we turned there were these red chinks in the darkness, and a lovely feeling of a whole town on the tiles.

'Where shall we go now?' Solomon said.

THE CARPENTER;

Or, the DANGER of EVIL COMPANY.

HERE was a young Weſt-country
man,
A Carpenter by trade;
A ſkilful wheelwright too was he,
And few ſuch Waggons made.

No Man a tighter Barn cou'd build,
Throughout his native town,
Thro' many a village round was he,
The beſt of workmen known.

His father left him what he had,
In ſooth it was enough;
His ſhining pewter, pots of braſs,
And all his houſehold ſtuff.

A little cottage too he had,
For eaſe and comfort plann'd,
And that he might not lack for ought,
An acre of good land.

A pleaſant orchard too there was,
Before his cottage door;
Of cider and of corn likewiſe,
He had a little ſtore.

Active and healthy, ſtout and young,
No buſineſs wanted he;
Now tell me reader if you can,
What man more bleſt cou'd be?

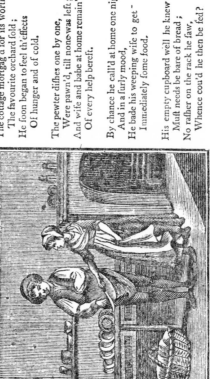

But vain and vicious was the ſong,
And wicked was the tale;
And every pauſe he always fill'd,
With cider, gin, or ale.

Our Carpenter delighted much,
To hear the Cooper talk;
And with him to the Ale-houſe oft,
Would take his evening walk.

The cottage mortgag'd for its worth,
The favourite orchard ſold;
He ſoon began to feel th' effects
Of hunger and of cold.

The pewter diſhes one by one,
Were pawn'd, till none was left;
And wife and babe at home remain'd
Of every help bereft.

By chance he call'd at home one nigh
And in a ſurly mood,
He bade his weeping wife to get -
Immediately ſome food.

His empty cupboard well he knew
Muſt needs be bare of bread;
No raſher on the rack he ſaw,
Whence cou'd he then be fed?

His wife* a piteous ſigh did heave,
And then before him laid
A baſket cover'd with a cloth
But not a word ſhe ſaid.

Then to her huſband gave a knife
With many a ſilent tear;
In haſte he tore the cover off,
And ſaw his child lay there.

The *Compleat Imbiber* has never failed to find room for the improving tract, and here presents one of **Mr.** Hazard's halfpenny broadsheets, composed in the late eighteenth century to persuade the poor to be temperate, so that the economy could be made secure for the Georgian four-bottle man and the Regency rake.

Was all for which he car'd;
But foon be drank as much as he,
To fwear like him foon dar'd.

His hammer now negleincluded lay,
For work he little car'd;
Half finifh'd wheels, and broken tools,
Were ftrew'd about his yard.

To get him to attend his work,
No prayers cou'd now prevail:
His hatchet and his plane forgot,
He never drove a Nail.

His chearful ev'nings now no more,
With peace and plenty fmil'd;
No more he fought his pleafing Wife,
Nor hugg'd his fmiling child.

For not his drunken nights alone,
Were with the Cooper paft;
His days were at the Angel fpent,
And ftill he flay'd the laft.

No handfome Sunday fuit was left,
Nor decent holland fhirt;
No nofegay mark'd the Sabbath day,
But all was rags and dirt.

No more his Church he did frequent,
A fymptom ever fad;
Where once the Sunday is mifpent,
The week days muft be bad.

Where is the Lord, or where the Squire,
Had greater caufe to praife,
The goodnefs of that bounteous hand,
Which bleft his profp'rous days?

Each night when he return'd from work,
His wife fo meek and mild,
His little fupper gladly drefs'd,
While he carefs'd his child.

One blooming babe was all he had,
His only darling dear,
The object of their equal love,
The folace of their care.

O what cou'd ruin fuch a life,
And fpoil fo fair a lot?
O what cou'd change fo kind a heart,
All goodnefs quite forgot?

With grief the caufe I muft relate,
The difmal caufe reveal,
'Twas EVIL COMPANY and DRINK,
The fource of every ill.

A Cooper came to live hard by,
Who did his fancy pleafe;
An idle rambling Man was he,
Who oft had crofs'd the feas.

This Man could tell a merry tale,
And fing a merry fong;
And thofe who heard him fing or talk,
Ne'er thought the ev'ning long.

He wrung his hands——confefs'd his fins,
And did both weep and pray.

From that fame hour the Cooper more,
He never wou'd behold;
Nor wou'd he to the Ale-houfe go,
Had it been pav'd with gold.

His Wife forgave him all the paft,
And footh'd his forrowing mind,
And much he griev'd that e'er he wrong'd
The worthieft of her kind.

By lab'ring hard, and working late,
By induftry and pains,
His Cottage was at length redeem'd,
And fav'd were all his gains.

His Sundays now at Church were fpent,
His home was his delight,
The following verfe himfelf he made,
And read it every night:

The Drunkard Murders Child and Wife,
Nor matters it a pin,
Whether he ftabs them with his knife,
Or ftarves them by his gin.

* See Berquin's Gardener.

[*Enter'd at Stationers Hall.*]

Z.

Sold by S. HAZARD, (PRINTER to the CHEAP REPOSITORY for Religious and Moral Tracts) at BATH;
By J. MARSHALL, PRINTER to the CHEAP REPOSITORY, PRINTER to the
Queen-Street, Cheap-Side, and No. 4, Aldermary Church-Yard; R. WHITE, Piccadilly, LONDON;
and by all Bookfellers, Newfmen, and Hawkers, in Town and Country.——Great Allowance will be made to Shopkeepers and Hawkers.

CHEAP REPOSITORIES No. 17,
Price an Half-penny, or 2s. 3d. per 100. 1s. 3d. for 50, 9d. for 25.

The Technique of Tasting

BY MICHAEL BROADBENT, M.W.

If you can taste food you can taste wine. However, a reasoned judgement must be based on knowledge, and knowledge of wine can only be acquired with the practice which is needed to develop a vinous memory.

There is no doubt that some people have a more delicate and sensitive palate than others, but this alone, without training, is less useful than a normal but well-trained palate. The more rarefied and literary flights of tasting expertise are of limited practical value and will be discounted in these notes.

THE REASONS FOR TASTING

All wine which passes the lips is 'tasted' whether or not a conscious comment or judgement is made. However, the word 'tasting' in this particular context refers to a deliberate act, the object of which is to assess the qualities of the wine in question.

Most tastings have, or should have, a practical aim:

(a) To examine the general balance and condition of the wine during the early stages of its development in cask or in bottle.

(b) To estimate the quality of a wine prior to purchase, whether it be by a broker from the grower, shipper from broker, merchant from shipper, or consumer from merchant (or hotelier).

(c) And the converse: to judge its maturity and value for selling purposes.

(d) To assess its suitability for a particular occasion, type of food or guest.

All tastings are valuable, but to a degree which varies proportionately with the care and understanding bestowed; and this in turn depends on real knowledge and genuine interest.

The most useful tastings are those of a comparative nature where wines of differing ages or districts can be tasted alongside one another.

This will depend partly on the reason for tasting:

(a) The buyer, with one eye cocked at the price and pedigree, will look for the physical components of the wine and its balance in the light of future requirements.

(b) The merchant will examine its general condition, latent stability and state of development.

(c) The salesman will look for attractive drinking qualities and value.

(d) The host will taste to see if the wine is ready for drinking (mature enough, the right temperature, etc.), whether it will complement the particular dish it is meant to accompany, and whether it is suitable for the time of day or season of the year, and finally whether it will be appreciated by his guests (there is nothing more heartbreaking than sharing a mature first-growth claret with someone who is incapable of appreciating its refinements and subtleties).

WHAT CATEGORY OF TASTER ARE YOU?

It follows that tasters in the different categories mentioned above will naturally tend to look for, and record, different aspects of a wine. A wine chemist, for example, will tend to interest himself in the alcoholic content, acidity, free sulphur and other factors which affect stability; the salesman will often ignore the physical composition of the wine, concentrating more on its sweetness or dryness and general 'drinkability' and value.

It may not be desirable to know every single thing about a wine, nor will time always permit it. However, there are obvious dangers in allowing the purely one-sided approach to become habitual.

WHEN TO TASTE

This depends on the reason and on the occasion.

Growers and merchants taste early or mid-morning when their palates are freshest. Outside the trade, tastings more often take place at lunchtime or in the early evening. The host will taste the wine prior to serving, generally before the guests arrive (only very delicate old wines need be decanted at the table—but this is another subject).

It is easier to say when one should *not* taste than when one should. For example, it is undesirable to taste immediately after any meal, or when one is tired. In the early morning, use water to rinse away remnants of toothpaste, or alkaline mouthwash, otherwise they will react on the wine in the mouth, making tasting both difficult and unpleasant.

SPECIAL POINTS TO NOTE

(a) Get into the habit of making notes even if they appear feeble or nonsensical at first. Remembering the name of a wine but forgetting its taste, or the opposite—which is commoner, as frustrated wine merchants know—is tiresome and unnecessary. The poorest memory will be well served by the briefest record of name, description and opinion.

(b) It is perfectly possible to judge one wine on its own, but its qualities will be thrown into perspective if it is tasted alongside another wine of slightly lesser or greater quality, or one from an adjacent district or different vintage year.

Better still are the comparative tastings of six or more wines. Differences of maturity, development, style and degree of quality and finesse can be assessed so much more readily. If you want to show off a really fine wine at a dinner party, precede it with a more modest wine of comparable style. The star qualities of the fine wine will appear to greater advantage.

(c) Taste the wines in the most appropriate order. For example:
Dry before sweet (this is essential).
Red before white (this is debatable. Some experts prefer to taste dry white wine before red, the order in which they are generally served during meals).
Young before old.
Modest before fine.

(d) For a completely objective assessment, taste wines 'blind'. Even the least impressionable and most experienced tasters are biased—unconsciously or otherwise—by the sight of the bottle and label. Taste a range of wines in numbered glasses. Failing this, turn the bottles round or cover them up.

(e) It is normal to examine the appearance of a wine, then smell it and finally taste it, in that order. However, when faced with a range of closely associated wines (for example ten wines from the Médoc of the same vintage) comparisons are speeded by looking at them carefully, moving up the line holding one against the other, then smelling each in turn, and lastly tasting them in the same ascending order.

Arrange your tasting sheets in advance so that an immediate note can be made in the correct place.

When tasting a range of wines in ascending quality, the lesser ones will be seen in sharper perspective if one dodges back to them after completing the line.

DETAILED INSTRUCTIONS FOR TASTING

The order in which one tastes a wine is based on the natural physical movement of the glass from table to mouth. First of all, the glass is picked up and looked at. This is stage one. As it is raised towards the mouth the nose catches the bouquet—stage two. Then the lips meet the rim of the glass and stage three, the tasting, commences.

What to look for during the three basic stages is detailed below.

STAGE ONE — APPEARANCE

Use a normal, tulip-shaped, clear wine glass and not a fancy, straight-sided, or coloured one.

If tasting a range of wines, use matching glasses of a generous size. Pour an equal measure in each so that the relative depth of hue can be seen at a glance. Do not fill the glass more than half-full as it will be easier to tilt over a white table top, an essential manœuvre if the informative colour at the rim of the wine is to be seen clearly.

Pick up the glass by its stem, not by the bowl. This makes it easier to examine the wine, particularly if held against a candle. It also has the virtue of avoiding sticky finger marks on the sides of the glass.

Daylight is best, as unnatural light can affect both the hue and tone. In particular avoid blue fluorescent, it makes red wine look unhealthily dark and blue tinged. Candle light is romantic: it enhances the appearance of both wine and lady guest! But for a serious tasting the only real use of a candle is to reveal the true clarity of a wine drawn from cask, or to show up bad decanting.

A. COLOUR

Most wines fall into one of three categories, red, white or rosé. But there is far more to it than that.

(i) Red Wines

What we know as a *red* wine will in fact vary in hue from deep purple through various prismatic shades of red to mahogany or even amber, depending mainly on the state of maturity, the vintage and the district.

Purple — indicates extreme youth or immaturity. Almost all red wines in cask will be this colour. They begin to lose their strong purple tinge in bottle, the length of time depending on their initial depth of colour.

Ruby — self-descriptive. The colour of a young port and not unlike that of a fullish claret or burgundy.

Red — by which we mean the colour approximating to 'claret', indicates the transitional period between youth and the acquisition of maturity and bottle age.

Red-Brown — in a table wine, indicates maturity (for example, claret with five or more years in bottle; burgundy three years or more, depending on the quality of the vintage).

Mahogany — a more mellow, subtle red-brown indicating considerable maturity (a claret with ten to twenty years' bottle age).

Tawny — a term, like ruby, usually associated with port. It describes a colour which has been attained either by blending or through loss of colour in cask, the former meeting style requirements, the latter being part of the natural maturing process.

Amber-Brown — indicates either a wine of very considerable age or one which is prematurely old and/or oxidised.

(ii) White Wines

So-called 'white' wines vary from the palest yellow/green through deeper shades of yellow to gold and deep amber brown.

Dry white wines usually start off life with little colour, and, unlike red wines, *gain* colour with age. Sweet wines generally start off a fuller shade of yellow, turn to gold and then take on a

190

brown tinge with age. Sherry is basically a pale-straw-yellow, some of the deeper shades being the result of ageing and blending. Practically all the dark oloroso and brown sherries gain their colour from added 'colour' wine of one sort or another.

Yellow-Green — a distinct green tinge is quite common in youthful white wines and is a particular, if not essential, characteristic of a Chablis or a young Moselle.

Straw-Yellow — a pleasant lively colour common to the majority of white wines, particularly the drier ones. In Burgundy, Meursaults tend to be more yellow than the Montrachets, and in Alsace, Traminers more yellow than Rieslings.

Yellow-Gold — quite a normal colour for any white wine but most frequently seen in the sweeter varieties such as Sauternes and hocks of *beerenauslese* quality.

Gold — generally indicates either a more lusciously sweet wine, or one with considerable bottle age (for example a white burgundy, usually pale straw when young, will develop a golden sheen after about six years in bottle).

Yellow-Brown or Old Gold — the colour of many dessert wines, fortified ones in particular. However a brown tinge in a white table wine indicates considerable bottle age, over-maturity or even oxidation. Many white burgundies will take on an un-healthy brown tinge after about twelve years in bottle; yet a fine Sauternes may not develop it for thirty years or more.

Maderised — this word is used to describe the appearance and condition of definite over-maturity and/or oxidation.

Brown — probably well past drinking (unless of course it is a sherry of that name or the tawny brown of an old wood port).

(iii) Rosé Wines

Wines described as rosé can vary enormously in colour and depth. Each district has its own style, depending on the type of grape used and on the method of making. The colour of a rosé is half its charm. A rosé wine is normally drunk young, for if it was allowed to age it would lose its freshness of colour and taste. There are exceptions: some begin life the colour of onion skin, a characteristic of those wines appropriately termed Pelure d'Oignon or Vin Gris.

Rosé — the perfect rosé should not look like a watered-down red wine, nor should it support an excess of orange or purple. It should be positive, clear and appealing—for the colour is its greatest attraction.

Orange — pure orange is not a desirable hue although a pleasant orange/pink is quite normal and characteristic of many rosés from the Loire and elsewhere.

Pink — a self-descriptive hue. Any suspicion of a blue tinge indicates unhealthiness, probably from bad fining or metallic contamination.

B. DEPTH OR TONE

Although the basic fullness or paleness of any wine will again depend to a certain extent on its origin, the relative depth will give a good indication of its physical content. For example, a very full, almost opaque, red/purple wine will almost certainly have more than its fair share of tannin and other natural properties. This depth, in association with the actual colour or hue, will give a clear indication of the maturity of the wine.

C. CLARITY

This is of prime importance in the various stages of development of all wines from time of fermentation and life in cask through to the time of bottling. Thereafter, white wines should be star bright and trouble free. Only reds normally throw a sediment in bottle.

The rather attractive silver tastevins which are sold in Burgundian souvenir shops (and used as ashtrays) are in fact traditional tasting vessels with a peculiar usefulness. The circular indentations in the shallow sides reflect candle light across the flat metal base to reveal at a glance the clarity of the new wine drawn from the cask in an ill-lit cellar. A tastevin is also more convenient to carry around and less fragile than a glass.

A dull cloudiness or obstinate haze of suspended matter in bottled wine is a bad sign and the wine should be returned to the supplier. Incidentally, think carefully before condemning a cloudy red wine. Was it recently sent through the post or carried up from the cellars hastily and clumsily?

Tiny pieces of floating cork are harmless; so are most forms of sediment which settle in the bottle easily. Bits of cork in the wine may be due to a bad corking machine or, more usually, through the careless use of a corkscrew. Wine with cork floating in it is *not* 'corked'—an ignorant misunderstanding which too often leads to completely fatuous and unnecessary complaints.

Flakes of tartaric acid crystals are sometimes seen in fortified and white wines. They are usually caused by a sudden change in temperature. These generally settle quickly and are also quite harmless and do not taste the wine.

STAGE TWO — NOSE OR BOUQUET

The importance and value of the nose or bouquet is generally underrated, for a great deal of valuable information about any wine can be gained from the smell alone. The first impression is generally the most telling. Deep breathing exercises do not help; on the contrary they tend to deaden the senses.

It is most difficult to analyse and describe most common or garden smells; even more so the subleties of a vinous bouquet. And if it is difficult to pin down the elements of a bouquet, it is almost impossible to convey them to another person. Some of the following characteristics are obvious and easily describable, some can only be recognised by an experienced 'nose'.

A. CLEANLINESS

Basically what is meant is that the wine should smell like wine, pure and unencumbered. Anything redolent of bad cabbages, old socks, vinegar, almond kernels, pear drops or any clearly extraneous or foreign smells, should be regarded as suspect, to say the least.

B. YOUTH OR AGE

The age of a wine can only be accurately judged on the nose by an experienced taster. The physical components of young wine tend to be pronounced and raw as they have had little time to settle down and blend together. Youthful acidity has a mouth-watering effect. A raw cooking apple smell indicates excess malic acid and is frequently found in young white wines, particularly in poorer vintage years.

As a wine mellows with age, its bouquet becomes noticeably softer and more harmonious. It takes on what is known as 'bottle age'. It is almost impossible to describe the smell called bottle age: on most white wines this shows up as a definable 'honeyed' quality; reds become richer and deeper. A wine with too much bottle age will exhibit its deterioration by taking on a flat, dull, toffee-like smell (maderised) or what is known as bottle stink (oxidation, a smell like bad cabbages).

C. FRUIT

'Fruit' is a desirable quality, but it should be noted that a wine can be described as fruity without having any trace of grapyness. A distinctly grapy bouquet is only found in wines made from certain unmistakable grape varieties (see glossary).

D. DEPTH

A bouquet can be described as light or deep, nondescript, superficial, full or rounded depending on the development of the wine. However care must be taken not to be misled by the 'full' bouquet of a ripe but poor quality wine or, conversely, by the 'dumb' or undeveloped bouquet of a very fine but immature wine.

(Other terms are listed under the heading 'bouquet' in the glossary.)

STAGE THREE — TASTE

The taste should generally confirm opinions drawn from the appearance and bouquet.

There are several points of oral contact which will reveal different taste characteristics—the tip of the tongue, the middle of the tongue, the roof of the mouth and the back of the throat. For this reason one tiny sip is usually inadequate. Take a reasonable mouthful, spit it out and repeat the process if necessary. The spitting side of tasting is one which causes the most guffaws amongst laymen. It is not necessary if there is only a very limited number of wines to taste; it is not advisable if there is no spittoon or if you are a bad shot. It is however essential if there is a large range of wines for, by swallowing the wine, successive tastes will become more and more blurred as the alcoholic content takes effect.

It is recommended that the elements which are detected on the palate are taken in strict order. It matters less what the order is than that the order is an habitual one. In this way one avoids overlooking certain features. The following is the order recommended by the writer:

A. DRYNESS OR SWEETNESS

A basic and easily judged constituent, particularly important in white wines. Do not be misled by thinness or excessive acidity which tends to make one under-estimate the actual sugar content or vice-versa (see glossary).

194

B. BODY
The 'weight' of wine in the mouth, basically due to its alcoholic content—an important binding and keeping element.

C. FLAVOUR
This is all important. Even if it is impossible to describe, at least record whether it is agreeable. The word 'typical' should be used sparingly.

D. ACIDITY
After dryness and flavour, acid is perhaps the most important and noticeable factor. It gives a wine purpose, 'zing' and finish. Extremes of acidity are, however, undesirable (see glossary). Excess sugar, natural or otherwise, tends to mask the true degree of acidity.

E. TANNIN CONTENT
Although disagreeable to the taste (it is harsh and dry in the mouth) it is an essential part of any young red wine. Tannin precipitates proteins and acts as a general preservative. It is essential for long life.

F. QUALITY, FINESSE, ELEGANCE, BREED
The elements of quality are represented by the completeness and balance of component parts. Quality can be judged by the length of time the flavour lingers in the mouth, by its richness and subtlety and by its aftertaste.

PRICE

Although not a 'tasting' quality, price is a factor which cannot often be ignored. It is certainly the common denominator of all wine-trade tastings except those concerned solely with the wine's physical development or condition.

Only a real wine snob or a hypocrite (often the same person) or a Gulbenkian need ignore the price factor altogether, though this does not mean that 'pure' or abstract tastings, comparing one wine with another, are not desirable, frequent or valuable. But for most purchasers and consumers of wine, price *is* the final arbiter in the sense that value for money is sought far more frequently than sheer quality.

Only two kinds of person can do without tasting notes; the rare and fortunate individual with a freak memory, and the less rare type who chooses not to complicate matters by ever tasting more than three firm favourites he knows and likes. (There is in fact a third: the really experienced specialist who spends every day tasting wines in his own particular field. For example the sherry or port blender. His highly developed palate for a comparatively limited range of smells and tastes may not require the support of the written word.)

Frankly any system is adequate that stores sufficient information for an individual's purpose in a speedily accessible manner.

The following information is more or less essential:

(a) The date of tasting.

(b) The name of the wine (district, vineyard).

(c) The vintage year (unless blended).

(d) If in bottle, the name of the bottler (if estate-bottled the name of the estate.) Château-bottlings merely require the qualifying initials (C.B.). If from the cask, write 'ex cask'.

(e) The price (per bottle, per dozen or per cask as appropriate).

(f) A description of the appearance of the wine.

(g) A description of its nose or bouquet.

(h) Its taste.

(i) General conclusions.

EXAMPLES

12/11/64. Château Beauregard, Pomerol, 1953, C.B.—retail 25s 6d. Appearance: red with distinct brown rim; medium deep; very clear (decanted—light loose sediment).

Bouquet: fine, clean, fruity, full and mature.

Palate: dryish, medium full-bodied; well-balanced (tannin and acid present but not predominant); excellent full flavour. Fine finish.

Conclusions: lovely wine, pleasant to drink now though with plenty of life left. Fair price.

17/10/64. Meursault, 1954, bottled by Bloggs & Co. Retail price
11s 6d.

Appearance: straw-gold, showing age; rather deep for a white
burgundy but star-bright.

Bouquet: fairly clean; remarkably youthful for its age though
acid is predominant as can be expected from an ageing 'off'.

Palate: dry; medium-full body; positive and attractive flavour
vintage.
Showing signs of age, the expected tiredness masked by considerable acidity which gives it a crisp finish.

Conclusions: old and fading but drinkable. Good value as a drink
but not a fair representative of the district.

CARD SYSTEM

Of the various methods of collating tasting notes the card system
has many virtues. A separate card for each wine is stored in
district, vintage or alphabetical order. This system is very handy
for quick reference. Appropriate sections can be extracted and
taken to the tasting room thus saving considerable time as headings are already prepared and do not have to be re-written.

CHRONOLOGICALLY ARRANGED TASTING BOOK

Notes are entered as the wines are tasted, in chronological order.
The advantage of this system is that a series of pocket-sized books
instead of a pack of cards can be used. The pages should be
ruled up vertically to save endless writing of main headings.

The disadvantages are the amount of writing required (details
of each wine have to be entered every time) and the need for an
accurate and up to date index to make quick reference possible.

LOOSE-LEAF TASTING BOOK

Like the card system, the wines can be kept in any order—
district, vintage or alphabetical. (This combines the virtues of
cards and books but tends to be bulky unless several wines can
be written up on one page.)

All methods require time, patience and an orderly mind (or an
obliging secretary with the same attributes). Like playing the
piano—many start, few continue. Like piano-playing it is worth
the effort in the long run, unless, of course, one is tone deaf!

In the section on the appearance of wine the various implications of colour, depth and clarity have been dealt with. These are in fact the easiest to describe because each element can be physically examined and compared with another. A colour can be pinned down pretty accurately—indeed in the blending of sherry colour matchings are obtained by using a spectrometer. The tone or depth can be judged quite easily and described objectively; and clarity is, for those with good eyesight and the aid of a good light, perhaps the easiest of all to assess and record.

But when it comes to describing smells and tastes we are entering the realms of subjective impressions, and even the most experienced taster may falter when it comes to expressing his reactions in words.

For this reason there has grown up a glossary of conventional terms which, by common usage in the trade and amongst most connoisseurs, goes some way towards pinning down tastes and smells, enabling them to be recorded so that they can be understood by other equally well-informed persons. The French, not unnaturally, have the most complete and expressive vocabulary on the subject and many of the current terms are literal translations. It is when we come to words like *sève* (lit: 'sap') that difficulties arise.

The following glossary is in two parts: the first deals with words used to describe the bouquet, the second with the various components of taste. Food and flower analogies such as those with truffles and violets, and abstract terms like 'voluptuous' and 'sensual' have been omitted. The former are self-explanatory, whilst the latter tend to be purely subjective and should really be reserved for the private ear or, if published, for the literary lushes. Unless a descriptive phrase *means* something and can be recognised afresh by its author, or better still, by a second party, it might as well be dispensed with.

WORDS USED TO DESCRIBE BOUQUET OR AROMA
Acetic — a distinctly vinegary smell as opposed to mere tartness. The wine will be undrinkable and past repair.
Almond kernels — (or almond paste) probably due to poor handling, bad fining. May well be drinkable, but not good.

Austere — severe, undeveloped. Often noticed on young fine
wines.

Baked — distinct smell of burnt and shrivelled grapes due to
excess sun and lack of rainfall.

Blackcurrants — the nearest fruit smell to the Cabernet Sauvignon grape. Particularly noticeable on wines from
Margaux and Pauillac.

Cedar — characteristic scent of many fine clarets.

Clean — absence of foreign odours.

Cooked — a resulting heavy sweet smell from over use of sugar
in poor vintages.

Deep — a bouquet of a full, rich and lasting quality as opposed
to a fragrant but superficial one.

Dumb — undeveloped, but with an inherent promise.

Fragrant — attractive and flowery.

Fruity — self-descriptive. A ripe, though not necessarily grapy
smell.

Grapy — a rich muscatel-like aroma produced by varieties of
that grape or by new varieties like Scheurebe and Müller-
Thurgau, etc. (Incidentally, all grape varieties have their
own characteristics: the Riesling, Sylvaner and Traminer
of Alsace and Germany all have distinct though related
smells; the Burgundian Pinot differs from Gamay and
both have characters distinctly different from the Cabernet
and Merlot of Bordeaux.)

Green — young and raw, exhibiting youthful acidity.

Little — scarcely any bouquet apparent. Either a dull ordinary
wine or an undeveloped one.

Meaty — heavy, rich, almost chewable quality.

Musty — self-explanatory. (Take heed: this may be due to stale
air in the bottle between cork and wine. If so, it will
wear off after a few minutes.)

Peardrops — occasionally noticeable on indifferently made wines
of lesser vintages. Unstable and in dubious condition.

Peppery — sharpness due to raw young component parts (alcohol,
acid, etc.) which have not had time to marry. Noticeable

on big young Rhône wines, on young ruby or immature vintage port and on many young full red wines.

Piquant — fresh and mouthwatering acidity. Desirable and customary characteristic of wines from the Moselle, Saar and Ruwer, also from districts like Sancerre.

Pricked — excess volatile acidity. Probably tart but may be *just* drinkable.

Spicey — a rich and subtle scent reminiscent of herbs and spices. A characteristic of Gewürztraminer.

Stalky — a smell of damp twigs, not necessarily derogatory, merely descriptive. Many young clarets have this rather evocative damp, chai-reminiscent smell.

Sulphury — a sharp acrid smell which prickles the back of the throat. Sulphur in one form or another is almost invariably used as an antiseptic, for cleaning casks and in mild solution to ensure the stability of *white* wines. Excesses are noticeable but not harmful.

Sweet — self-explanatory (note, however, that a dry wine can have a sweet smell).

Tart — a trifle over-acid. Similar to 'piquant' but probably too acid for the average layman. In a young wine it may wear off after further maturing time.

Woody — a particular aroma derived from the cask. Due to late racking, or contact with a poor quality cask or fresh raw new one, or just too much time in cask before bottling.

Volatile — bouquet is the result of volatile acids, esters and aldehydes. However an *excess* of volatile acidity is a danger sign, leading to acetification.

WORDS TO DESCRIBE TASTE, FLAVOUR AND GENERAL EFFECT IN THE MOUTH

Acid — an essential natural component which can be detected on the tongue. Acid is not only a preservative but gives a wine its essential 'bite' and provides bouquet. Degrees of acidity vary. It is high in Moselle and Saar wines and is responsible for their refreshing qualities. It is low in wines of some of the hotter and more southerly regions such as Algeria, southern Italy and southern Spain.

Lack of acidity results in a flabby wine with a watery finish; excess acidity results in a barely drinkable tartness or leads to a completely undrinkable acetification. Youthful acidity tends to mellow in the bottle and the wine is therefore likely to improve with keeping.

There are in fact several types of acid found in wine, some beneficial, others detrimental. The professional expert needs to know the difference but the subject is too complicated to be dealt with here.

Balance — the combination of natural components. See 'well balanced'.

Bite — a combination of tannin and acid. To be expected in a young wine but unpleasant if found in excess. Should wear off and mellow as the wine matures.

Bitter — a sign of ill-health probably due to undesirable acids or metallic contamination (take care though, the remnants of an alkaline toothpaste or the acidity of certain fruits can cause a similar effect).

Body — the weight of wine in the mouth due principally to the alcoholic content. This varies with the quality of the wine (and vintage), its style and its origin. It tends to be heavier in the south (e.g. the Rhône) than the north (Moselle).

Breed — a quality stemming from the wine's parentage (both vineyard and vigneron, the site and soil of the one and the skill of the other).

Cloying — sweet and heavy. Lacking acidity to make it crisp and interesting.

Coarse — rough, of poor parentage and possibly indifferently made. Do not confuse coarseness of character with the rough rawness of a fine but immature young wine.

Delicate — a light and charming quality.

Depth — a desirable quality implying a multiplicity ('layers') of flavour.

Dry — absence of sugar (fully fermented out).

Fat — medium to full bodied, with a soft rounded texture.

Fruit — a fleshy quality derived from ripe grapes, but not necessarily 'grapy' in flavour.

Full-bodied — filling the mouth. High alcoholic content probably over 13° G.L. (i.e. 13 per cent alcohol by volume).

Finish — a pleasing and firm end to the taste, resulting from a healthy and appropriate degree of acidity. A wine cannot be considered well-balanced without a good finish. A poor finish is watery and inconclusive and is a sure sign of lack of acidity, general imbalance and poor quality.

Grapy — a distinctive flavour derived from the use of certain grape varieties such as Muscat or Muscatelle and from relatively new crossings like Müller-Thurgau or Scheurebe.

Grip — firm and emphatic combination of physical characteristics (as opposed to flabbiness or spinelessness).

Green — youthful acidity which will wear off as the wine gains maturity.

Hard — an easily detected severity due to over-prominence of tannin and acid, both of which may mellow in time.

Heavy — full-bodied and overpowering. Take care to watch the context; a strapping Rhône wine would suit a gargantuan dinner in the middle of winter but would appear heavy and overpowering at a light summer luncheon.

Light — implying lack of body. Probably under 12° G.L.

Luscious — soft, sweet, fat and fruity—all in balance.

Medium body — probably 12-13° G.L.

Medium dry — containing a small quantity of natural sweetness but probably dry enough to be drunk before or during a meal.

Medium sweet — distinctly on the sweet side though not sweet enough for a dessert wine. Probably too sweet to drink with the main course of a meal unless you have a sweet tooth.

Piquant — a degree of refreshing acidity which makes the mouth water—desirable in many light, dry white wines but not in others.

Rich — a full, but not necessarily sweet, ensemble of fruit, flavour and body.

Robust — full bodied and rounded. A good strapping mouthful of a wine.

Sap — the quality of inherent life that will help develop a young wine (*sève* in French).

Severe — hard and immature. Either a big, young undeveloped wine or one showing an unnatural excess of tannin and acid.

Silky — a firm yet soft texture on the palate. One of the

characteristics of a fine Pomerol.

Soft — agreeable texture in the mouth, at its best promising a certain maturity and balance. However a soft *young* wine may lack guts and keeping power.

Superficial — not unattractive but without depth or real quality.

Supple — easy to feel, hard to define: combining sap, vigour and a distinct but amenable texture.

Sweet — a wine with a high sugar content. Essential element of any dessert wine.

Tannin — tannin dries the roof of the mouth and grips the teeth. It is an essential preservative derived from the grape during fermentation but is broken down and becomes mellow with age. Very noticeable in many young red wines, particularly claret.

Tough — a full bodied wine of overpowering immaturity (not necessarily youthful) probably with an over-high tannin content.

Vigorous — lively, healthy and positive flavour associated with youthful development.

Well-balanced — satisfactory blend of physical components (fruit, alcohol, tannin, acid) and the less tangible elements (breed, character, finesse, etc.).

Twenty Years of Latour—

a Tasting in California

BY WILLIAM DICKERSON

Some of the most knowledgeable tasting of wine, and some of the best-informed writing about it, now goes on in the United States: Dr. Dickerson is one of a band of distinguished Californian amateurs who—like many New Yorkers— command the resources enabling them to experience the greatest French and German wines, and the taste and judgment to appreciate and enjoy them. And it is only by experiencing the best that it is possible to set standards by which to judge other, more modest, wines.

In considering this scholarly account of a comparative tasting of some of the most important years of a great first-growth claret, the English reader should bear in mind that, as Edmund Penning-Rowsell observes in the article that follows this, European wines 'come on' more quickly in the United States than in Europe. It may be that they come on more quickly in California than on the eastern seaboard. So the same years tasted in England might well take up different relative positions because of the different rate of maturation: two footnotes indicate such possible differences. C.R.

he tasting 'to compare the progress and development of the recent vintages of the Château Latour' was carefully planned and conducted by Walter Peterson. To do so, he acquired 15 vintages and 10 guests. The wines (more difficult to collect than the tasters) comprised the following vintages: 1959, 1958, 1957, 1956, 1955, 1953, 1952, 1951, 1950, 1949, 1948, 1947, 1945, 1941, and 1937.

The guests recorded personal observations about each wine and ranked all the wines according to their individual preferences.

Ranking any disparate wines, even from the same vineyard, on a single scale has obvious limitations, and here a robust young wine had to be compared with a senior companion mellowed by an advantage of 22 years.

Despite such difficulties all tasters were forced to assign a single numerical rating to each wine. These ratings showed some differences but surprisingly few major discrepancies. The individual rankings were then combined and the group consensus is presented here. To describe these wines in greater detail the independent opinions of only two members (the host and the author) are included.

Those vintages comparing least favourably on this occasion were the 1956, good colour with a dry earthiness in the bouquet and a pleasant but unsustaining finish to the taste, and the 1941 which was typical of Latour. Reminded of the awesome handicaps of 1941 by the clear glass of the bottle and the short cork, we were thankful to have any wine of that year available, regardless of its shortcomings. Ranked 13th was 1957, a wine already well-described by Mr. Waugh.* The 1947, representing a year of such

*Mr. Harry Waugh, of Harveys, and a director of Château Latour, in an article in 'Wine and Food' (No 118, Summer, 1963) described the 1957 as having good colour and flavour, but retaining the tannin and immaturity typical of its year, and not ready to drink. But he was reporting a tasting held in November 1962 and, as I have already mentioned, wine comes on more quickly in the United States than in Europe. C.R.

general great promise, proved a disappointing 12th; handicapped particularly in the nose and in the aftertaste. Next came the 1948, showing a slight brown at the edge and with the bouquet lighter and the flavour less well-balanced than the excellent Latours yet to be listed.

Placed tenth was 1958, a promising young wine with fruitiness in the bouquet, good body and acidity, ample tannin and surely an exciting bottle for future tables. The 1950, despite a flaky sediment which packed harder than any other, was still not completely brilliant in colour and the typical Pauillac nose was offset by a slight cask odour, a wine to drink rather than keep. Eighth in excellence was the 1952, a proud dark wine with a big and 'aged' bouquet possessing good flavours and fine balance. Barely ahead

was 1951, already a wonderful wine but with sufficient tannin to offer further development and to beg for more patience.

All the remaining bottles showed the elegance, the breeding, and the excellence looked for in those great wines which have earned and maintained the reputation of Château Latour. The 1953 was a dark handsome wine of good bouquet that proved its real merit in the mouth*. The taste was superbly smooth, even and round. 'It fills the mouth and is a wine that demands chewing.' Ranked next was the 1937 but those who favour older vintages, including both commentators quoted, placed it much higher. The lack of a perfect brilliance was the only fault in this bottle. The robe remained a rich red. The bouquet was well-developed, generous, and continued to show some fruit-like qualities. Beautifully balanced and enticingly complex, it was a true champion without fatigue.

The 1955, dark red to the eye, was a delight to the nose—rich with fruitiness, aromatic with perfumes and abounding with Cabernet odours, and bottle bouquet. Still developing, it possessed everything needed to make an outstanding and characteristic claret.

Third position was granted the most junior challenger, the 1959. Its youth was apparent in the slight blue tinge, in the high fruitiness and freshness, and in the richness of flavours: all need time to mature. Not heavy but displaying an early finesse, the wine appeared to be developing complexity rather than great body.

Second choice was a truly superb wine—robust but subtle, velvet yet with great life, finesse, and a pleasant lingering finish, all in perfect balance. A very great bottle and a tribute to the Château was the 1949.

Offered pride of place was the 1945. The colour had an edge of slight brown. An initial presence in the bouquet and the taste, thought to be a volatile acid, disappeared in a short time and was soon forgotten in the enormous enjoyment of this magnificent wine. When praised above such competition, what more need be said of the 1945?

*At a tasting of the three first-growth 1953 Médocs in London early in 1965—more recently than the American tasting recorded here—Mr. Harry Waugh, Mr. Robin McDouall of the Travellers' Club, and the editor all found the Latour, 'still unyielding', as the editor recorded at the time, 'the tannin masking its charm'. Mr. Waugh's opinon was that it needed another four or five years. On that occasion it was the Margaux that bore away the palm.

C.R.

What to Buy and Drink in 1966

BY EDMUND PENNING-ROWSELL

HE old joke of the Christmas-card artist, sitting under a midsummer sun, with the sweat pouring from him, as he paints the snowscape, surely applies to this contributor to *The Compleat Imbiber*. For the time involved in producing a book is not much less than that involved in producing a bottle of wine; and those Bordeaux merchants who speculate on the coming vintage by buying *sur souche* in May or June are backing certainties compared with the task of estimating the development of many different types of wine in 1966. For wine is often unpredictable; hence much of its interest.

Certainly, wine merchants are often credited—by their customers —with uncanny powers of prediction; and on their side these wine experts do not always disavow such prophetic gifts. Peering at, if not through, their glasses darkly, they say firmly, 'this wine should be at its best in another eighteen months'. The skilful placing of this ranging shot takes the amateur by storm; not a year, mark you, or two years, but just exactly in between. Who knows how long after that calculated peak the wine will stay *à point*? The wine-prophet's customer, burdened with five dozen Château X, a hard little Médoc *cru bourgeois* of, say, the 1957 vintage, foresees a crowded succession of lunch parties, dinner parties, wine and cheese parties and even picnics devoted to Château X's brief flowering before its descent into undrinkability and the kitchen sink.

The experts are not always so pontifical, nor do they always mean their words to be taken too literally—as for example those who say that we should not start 'looking at' the 1961s until the early 1980s. The facts are that no one knows, and every vintage in northern Europe is different. Attempts to establish rhythmic patterns based on vintages a century ago, on comet years or on even or odd numbered vintages have been no more successful than systems evolved to beat the bank at Monte Carlo. If it is certainty one wants with wine, then one drinks it from countries with generally equable weather conditions, such as Greece, Italy, California and Australia. There the progress of a wine may be fairly charted, and the chief point of vintage labels—when accurate—is to indicate age.

White wine prospects are easier to estimate than red, for they may be drunk younger, and their life span tends to be shorter, except for certain of the more luscious wines.

My view is that with wines which benefit from ageing, particularly red wines, development is much slower than often believed; once mature they stay at a peak for quite a long time, and then decline not sharply but slowly. To take an example of a senior and famous claret vintage, people have been saying for nearly twenty years that the 1929 clarets were 'past their best'. This is certainly true of some of them now; but wines sometimes recover their balance. I remember in the late 1940s exchanging one or two red Graves of this vintage, as they seemed to be losing their fruit. Since then I have drunk some admirable bottles of these same wines. Much depends on where and how a wine has been kept and, I suggest, how often it has been moved. Not long ago I drank a bottle of Château Margaux 1929, château-bottled and from a case bought at auction not long before. It was thin, lacking in fruit and altogether disappointing. But a few months later, in the offices of an old-established City of London wine merchant, I drank the same wine. It had scarcely been moved in 30 years, and each of the three bottles served was delicious. All in all there are still fine 1929 clarets to be found, as I was recently reminded by a magnum of Château Gruaud Larose.

Again, in 1940 Maurice Healy in *Stay Me With Flagons* described Château Latour 1920 as 'precocious'. Maybe it was, but today, a quarter of a century later, Château Latour is probably the finest wine of that vintage. So the utterances of vintage chartists and wine prophets, professional and amateur, should be treated with reserve; like the pianist, they are doing their best.

It should also be borne in mind that wine develops differently according to country. It seems clear that French wine ages more rapidly in the United States than in Britain, owing to the higher and more variable temperatures; this apart from wines lovingly preserved in air-conditioned apartments at 70 degrees Fahrenheit.

Maurice Healy remarked that 'wines mature more quickly in Bordeaux than in England.' This may be so in the warmer climate, and when much of the wine is stored above ground. But it is also true that, subject to little movement, they can last longer there. On my last visit I drank Château Mouton Rothschild 1940 (a magnum), and at Château Latour the next day I tasted their 1940. This was a light year of no great reputation, but in each case they were true and fruity to the end. I doubt however whether either would have been so good if moved far in old age.

The moral is that when buying old wines in 1966 or in any other year, try to find out where they have been kept and, if possible, taste before buying.

When buying young red wines, you should not under-estimate your requirements, but acquire enough to test, periodically, a wine's development. The really expensive wines, such as Bordeaux *premiers crus*, may have to be bought sparingly and taken on trust, but with the general run of red wines, if a wine is worth buying, then it is worth buying a dozen bottles at least. As few wines may be found on a merchant's list for more than two or three years, the first purchase may be the last. So even with a case of a wine, one will—to state a fact less clearly obvious at the moment of purchase than several years later—only be able to drink this wine a dozen times, and less than that if more than one bottle is opened on any single occasion. The wine in question may take seven to ten years after purchase to mature, and thereafter last another ten years. If the wine turns out as well as hoped, it is a thin spread over a decade of drinking, especially as one or two bottles are almost certain to have been drunk during its development.

White wine, readier sooner and shorter-lived, is less of a problem, and smaller quantities may be bought with the hope of early re-ordering. Yet if fine single-vineyard wines are being bought, from German estates or Burgundy single vineyards, it is well to remember that original quantities are not large, and your merchant may not have large supplies.

The exact quantity to be bought of a young wine will obviously depend not only on your drinking habits but also on your spread of purchases. There are those who select a Beaujolais, burgundy or claret of a good vintage and buy a good bin-full, for regular drinking in three, five or ten years ahead. Others will prefer to spread their risk and interest and buy widely in much smaller quantities. I personally am of the latter category, for apart from not wanting to put all my eggs into one bin, I like to represent a vintage in one area as comprehensively as possible. For example in buying a burgundy vintage, it would be agreeable to start with a modest Santenay at one end of the Côte and finish up with a Chambertin at the other end. On the way call for a purchase of Volnay or Pommard, and possibly both, and certainly a Beaune—perhaps from the Grèves or Marconnets vineyards. Skirting the Aloxe-Cortons, which I personally find rather tough, I would look for a good second-rank Nuits St. Georges—this can be an admirable wine for second-rank occasions—and pass on to Vosne, Flagey-Echézeaux, Chambolle and Gevrey, with at least a sample named growth from each and perhaps two or three from star-studded Vosne. Although Clos de Vougeot and Morey have been by-passed, it will be seen that not far short of a dozen dozen—assuming a basic case apiece—have been bought of this one vintage en route. Like other ideals it may be unattained, and there are the white burgundies to consider as well, and probably the clarets over in Bordeaux, but at least this is a pattern.

It will be seen that in principle I favour buying wines when young, for then they are cheaper and in greatest variety. Nowadays it is not practical to postpone all buying until clarets and red burgundies are approaching maturity. The problem of how much to buy is always complicated by the uncertainty of what the next vintage and the one after will be like. This in diminished form, is the problem much more acutely faced by every wine merchant, especially today, when older wine stocks are slim and early purchase decisions have to be made in the wine districts.

For the private buyer, the decision is easier, for at least he will have had early views on the prospects of the next two vintages. For example, the buyer of 1961 clarets, when first listed in 1964, was aware of the success of the 1962s and 1964s and the failure of the 1963s. As a rough guide, it may be said that Bordeaux produces at least five good vintages in a decade, Burgundy not more than four, and it would be unsafe to count on more than two or three good German wine years in ten. Champagne runs more or less level with Burgundy; Alsace is more even; and the rest of France, including the Loire and Rhône, swing between the Burgundy and Bordeaux patterns. But, to avoid 'chartist' accusations, I must point to the 1930s, when only two or three grudgingly good years turned up and at least six very bad vintages. At the moment it should be borne in mind that the 1960s have already accounted for three good years in the main French areas: 1961, 1962 and 1964. So we may be in for some lean years; and a good young vintage wine in the bin is worth several in prospect. In these inflationary times the earlier vintage may well be cheaper, and in any case it has the advantages of seniority and advancing maturity.

This article deals not so much with the odd bottle bought off the rack, but with those bought with thought for the future, notably claret, red burgundy and the finer white wines. Therefore before dealing with particular vintages, a few general comments on buying these categories may be of use.

BUYING CLARET

First determine your likes and priorities. Do you like Médocs, red Graves, or St. Emilions and Pomerols? Perhaps you like them all, although most people have a leaning one way or another. If it is towards delicacy and lightness you may prefer Médocs, if for refinement coupled with a certain austerity then the red Graves are admirable, but if you like big fruity wines you may first choose St. Emilions and Pomerols. These last have the advantage of maturing earlier than many Médocs and Graves, but lack their distinction as well as what wine experts call 'breed'. Médocs themselves break down into types, from the elegant Margaux and delicate but fruity St. Juliens, to the powerful Pauillacs and tough St. Estèphes.

Secondly, take some advice as to which are the most reliable vineyards in your price range. Of course they vary, but certain châteaux have a good reputation and others not so good. I am constantly surprised by the number of *crus classés* that produce indifferent wine.

Thirdly, consider whether you want to buy English-bottled or château-bottled clarets, or a proportion of either. The latter may cost you a few shillings a bottle more,* and first growths are all château-bottled. Is the extra worth it? For special occasions, I think it is. For although English merchants probably bottle better than most châteaux, there is the incalculable factor of the voyage, with the wine badly shaken and exposed to varying temperatures and possible oxidisation.

*There is only fivepence more in duty, but carriage and insurance are higher for wines imported in bottle, and there is usually a little extra profit along the line. C.R.

Generalisation is difficult owing to the variation between one proprietor and another in cultivation of the vineyards, in vinification and then in care of the wines in cask. Then there is the variation in 'house style' among the Côte d'Or merchants, who are responsible for nearly all the burgundy trade. To illustrate this, a distinguished London merchant has written; 'It is depressing that in these days the character of any *vin de commune* from the Burgundy district depends very much more on the shipper than on its locality'. Recommending and buying burgundy is, therefore, a tricky business. The best that can be said is that over-sweet coarse red burgundies are suspect, and over-suave ones too. Remember the vignerons of Dijon who, over a hundred years ago, demonstrated against the sugaring of burgundy, and declared that burgundy was a 'delicate' wine. A fine burgundy should have delicacy as well as a certain fruity fullness. So look for wines that are fragrant and fruity, but not too rich or over-powerful. Nor after a few years in bottle need they have a very deep colour. Burgundy, it should always be remembered, is not unfortified port.

Some people recommend buying only from certain shippers of reputation, and certainly some maintain a very high standard; but in most cases one has to pay fairly highly for that reputation. Others suggest buying French-bottled burgundies. The Americans, who import exclusively in bottle, are stressing domaine-bottling, in the belief that this way they secure authentic wine comparable with the château-bottling of Bordeaux. In fact domaine-bottling is virtually impossible in the vast majority of the small properties along the Côte d'Or. This will be appreciated by anyone who has visited one of the small cellars lying below these golden slopes. A relatively large concern like the Domaine de la Romanée Conti can practise domaine-bottling, along with a few others. But even the famous Montrachet Marquis de Laguiche is not domaine-bottled, but taken to Beaune where it is bottled by Joseph Drouhin, a merchant house; and none the less good for that. Many of the growers lack space for more than one year's wine in cask, and no facilities exist for bottling. The merchant firms can do all this better. The fact that some of them resort to undesirable practices is not solved by domaine-bottling. Burgundy-buying is a matter best discussed with your wine merchant—over a glass of another blended wine: sherry.

This is an omnibus heading, but there are certain points of general application. White wines are more difficult to look after than red wines, and more likely to be adversely affected by travel. So at wines at or above the £1 level they are probably best bought bottled at source. This also applies to low-strength wines like Pouilly Fumé and Sancerre, both from the Loire, and to Moselles. Nearly all fine German wines are estate-bottled, and when buying these one should look for the proprietor's name on the wine list. Broadly speaking, freshness of aroma and flavour, coupled with a pale colour, are the first considerations, although luscious Sauternes may be more golden. But a deep tinge is a sure sign of actual or approaching decline. White burgundies are subject to the same hazards as the reds, and there are even fewer of them. Apart from the really great sweet wines of France and Germany, it is unnecessary to buy white wines for drinking more than three or four years ahead, at most.

Coming to details, the vintage first to consider for buying in 1966 will be 1962, by then with a year or so in bottle. After the very high price of the 1961 clarets, the 1962 Bordeaux will immediately be welcomed for their more reasonable cost. The best wines are surely the Médocs. I tasted them on the spot when nearly two years old, and more recently after bottling in Britain. They seem forward, well-balanced but not full-bodied like the 1961s. The château-proprietors have a high opinion of them, and some suggest they will turn out like the 1953s. If so, no one will complain. The St. Emilions and Pomerols, with one or two exceptions, strike me as rather run-of-the-mill, sound, unexciting wines. The Pomerols lack that rich concentration of nose and flavour that is their great charm. Although a supporter of château-bottling I was somewhat alarmed to find it in progress during the very hot weather in the Médoc in the summer of 1964. But I am glad to say that the first growths, and châteaux like Léoville Barton, Palmer and Cantemerle were postponing it until the turn of the year in the traditional way, and no doubt other châteaux too, but the early, hot-bottled 1962s I shall taste with a certain apprehension.

The 1962 burgundies are also lighter than the 1961s, and promise to be drinkable earlier, with all the attractive, soft, fruity qualities of good burgundy. The crop was variable, and much therefore

depends on where and whom the wine came from; the best are
likely to be delicious. The white wines may lack some of the
crispness of the excellent 1961s. But with the 1963s a failure and
some at least of the 1964s likely to be acid-deficient, 1962 is not a
year to be passed over by white-burgundy drinkers.

Unfortunately, the 1962s are not a substitute for the high-
priced 1961 clarets, for these are certainly finer than any of their
neighbouring vintages, with a great deal of body and fruit, but
not, I hope, as backward-seeming as some believe. Even Château
Latour, traditionally a slow developer, and often actively disagreeable in its prolonged youth, produced a 1961 which shows some
flexibility, although not so forward as Château Haut Brion and
Château Margaux. After the original revulsion of trade and consumers at the high prices of the vintage—not so different, it
turned out, from the feeling three years later about the much
more plentiful but hardly as good 1964s—there has been a growing
demand for 1961s. Only the top growths are at sky-high prices;
the lesser wines are not too expensive. There is no doubt that this

is a claret vintage to be bought. But the sweeter white Bordeaux seems not so good as in 1959.

The 1961 burgundies have the advantage of being plentiful and thus not relatively dear. They are wines of powerful character and firmness. They could turn out to be very long-lived wines —if we let them. The whites are particularly fine, with more fruit than the 1957s and more acidity than the 1959s.

The 1959s suffered from an excess of publicity as well as of sun, and in the reaction against the former their reputation declined temporarily among more sophisticated wine-drinkers. Some wines certainly suffered from lack of acidity, and I have never cared for the white burgundies, although there are fine exceptions. And many of the German wines were disappointing for the same reason, the exceptions here being mostly in the Rheingau, Saar and Ruwer. Some of the clarets are maturing quickly, others are surprisingly backward and strong, almost coarse; they were relatively high in alcohol. The red burgundies are of course much softer, and so are being drunk up rapidly—

not least on the Côte d'Or itself, as I have witnessed. There is no reason to believe that either clarets or burgundies will have short lives, and in the light of later vintages and, in claret, of prices, 1959 is certainly a year to lay down in depth, if this has not already been done.

Older years to buy are growing scarce. The red burgundies of 1957 and 1955 are certainly worth considering; the former in particular are powerful, firm wines and should last well. So should the 1952s, but they are becoming very rare. The 1957 clarets are showing signs of softening as they approach the end of their first decade, but the 1955s are more agreeable; both vintages to be bought, but with care.

The classic years have here been mentioned, but off-year clarets are now spreading across the Channel and are worth considering. This has arisen owing to the shortage and prices of the fine years. Also the now legal sugaring at the time of fermentation has saved some Bordeaux vintages, from 1951 onwards. Consequently the 1960s and 1958s are now to be found here, and no doubt even a few 1963s will arrive in due course. In my view the 1958s are much superior to the 1960s, with Château Cantemerle, Château Latour, and Château Mouton Rothschild particularly attractive. The 1960s may gain some body in bottle, and they are worth the attention of those without older wines, or who are rightly unwilling to drink finer wines prematurely. Château Palmer and Château Latour are among the best 1960s.

It was at Château Latour that I had the most interesting off-vintage tasting of my life. In spite of its legalisation the *maître de chai* told me that sugaring was little employed at Latour, and not even in 1963. At this tasting bottles were opened of the following off-years: 1956, 1954, 1951, 1946, 1944, 1941, 1940, and 1939. All but the 1956, an edgy, hard wine, I found acceptable, although the 1941 and 1939 were, not altogether surprisingly, showing their age. *The surprise to me was the 1946—virtually unknown, standing between the famous 1945 and 1947. Rounded and fruity, it still had room for development. (These epithets might, I suggest, be applied to *The Compleat Imbiber* itself, and a second surprise, happily confirming my opinion in the *chai* of the château, was to have this wine served at the dinner given by Harveys to the contributors of the last issue.) The *maître de chai*

* Compare the Californian tasting reported by Dr. Dickerson: it is especially interesting to note the unanimity about the 1956. C.R.

himself preferred the 1951, but agreed that the 1946 was more complete. The 1954 was good, too. Separately we tasted the 1963 and it certainly seemed more like claret in embryo than some of the other Médocs, including first growths, tasted on this visit.

Buyers of German wines will now be able to estimate the quality of the 1964s. These are exceptionally plentiful, but also suffered from excessive heat, and so may be flabby, like some 1959s. As in 1921, some of the best wines may come from the normally less favoured sites, which on the Rhine and Moselle usually means the less sunny sites in that northern wine region. In 1964 less sun may mean better wines. On the other hand the normally sun-and-heat-deficient Saar and Ruwer wines may, as with the 1959s, be the best buys for the 1964s, along with the main Moselle and the Rheingau wines. There is no doubt that this is the best opportunity for buyers of German wine since 1959; and such opportunities are not all that common for those who drink above the Liebfraumilch level.

Another set of wine drinkers who should seize their opportunity in 1966 are those dedicated to vintage port. Although its drinking is commonly mourned as being in decline, in fact mature vintage port is very much in short supply. One expert recently declared that by 1970 there would be no more of it. Although I do not follow the basis of his calculations, there is no doubt that it is being drunk much younger than it used to be. Even in our senior university common rooms there are nightly massacres of port scarcely more than a dozen years old; and the traditional score of years for maturing is everywhere breached. True, some ports that have been declared as vintage have been very light, such as 1947 and 1950; and no doubt the port producers will not be entirely immune from the tendency to produce quick-maturing wines. Certainly the new young vintage ports are in demand as soon as offered, and it may be that in the measurable future the only people who have mature vintage port will be the institutional buyers who lay it down as soon as it is bottled, and private consumers who take the plunge at or near the same time, keeping it below stairs or in their merchants' cellars Now that 1963 has been declared a vintage year—the first since 1960—the chance has arrived to buy at opening prices. Even if you feel disinclined to take the plunge to the extent of the traditional pipe—54 dozen bottles, costing initially about £650, duty paid—a modest six or ten dozen would provide a brave sight over the years in anyone's cellar. Even if one could not drink it all, vintage port is still probably the best investment in wine.

When it comes to what to drink in 1966, the exercise is briefer but not less difficult. Indeed some find the decision as to what wine to open harder than what to acquire. Is Château X ready yet, or should we wait another year or so? Is Clos Y good enough or too good for old So-and-So? It is difficult, I find, to open a leading wine, such as a Médoc *premier cru*, on family occasions only, and yet some of the visitors may appreciate them less; the best bottles await the appreciative guest, and some may wait all too long. But there are those, more generous to themselves, who drink their best bottles *en famille* and leave the Beaujolais for visitors.

The most enjoyable claret vintage to drink now is surely 1953, and good luck to those who bought them in 1956-8 at what now seem knock-down prices. They are deliciously soft, forward wines, particularly the Médocs. At the top of the list I would put Château Lafite, Château Palmer, Château Margaux, Château Mouton Rothschild and Château Léoville Barton. But the level of excellence is high, down to some of the fine bourgeois growths. The red Graves are delicious too, including Château La Mission Haut Brion and Château Pape Clément. If the Pomerols and St. Emilions are often not quite as good as the firmer 1952s, they are still very attractive.

My next choice—in say, a friend's cellar of postwar vintages—would be 1949, still rather a powerful, and sometimes 'edgy' vintage, but I would expect it to be smoother by 1966. But an alternative might be 1948, that excellent if neglected vintage. Among the winners are Châteaux Cheval Blanc, La Mission Haut Brion, Brane Cantenac and Léoville Barton. If then restricted to St. Emilions and Pomerols I would plump for 1952—with some remarkably fine wines, the only fault in which is a certain hardness that might decrease. Château Pétrus and Château Cheval Blanc are the leaders. They too are among the better wines still of 1950, a medium year which has hung on remarkably well, but which should certainly not be kept. Château Ausone, often a little disappointing nowadays, is a good 1950, if château-bottled.

In 1966 I shall expect to drink 1958 rather than 1957 clarets, and, perhaps 1960s rather than 1959s—preserving the more long-lived years.

From the 'museum bin' I would drink 1947s, and particularly

expect to enjoy the better St. Emilions and Pomerols, notably
Château Cheval Blanc and Vieux Château Certan. And I would
hope that the 1945s, having now reached their majority, would
also have attained maturity.

My first burgundy vintage choice would be 1949, and occasionally, if the bottles are right, 1947. For quality, however, the finer
1953s, particularly the Côte de Nuits wines, might run them close;
the Côte de Beaune wines tend to lack stamina. For more ordinary
drinking, 1955 is almost certainly the best year; not great, but
what one might call agreeably accommodating wines. The 1952s,
although quite drinkable, seem to me wines still for keeping, but
the Pommards, Volnays and Beaunes less so. The 1957 Côte de
Beaune wines are also more forward than the Côte de Nuits.
There is no harm but also no hurry in drinking them. The more
forward of the 1959s should make very attractive, fruity burgundies
by the time they are seven years old. As off-vintages of red
burgundies are seldom shipped they need not be considered, but
it is to be hoped that their absence will not lead to a premature
assault on the 1961s.

Among white burgundies, the excellent 1961s should still be
at their best after five years, and, if French-bottled and fine,
ought to last several years thereafter. Eight to ten years is the
normal limit for the best white burgundies. The next year is
1962, softer and less incisive. There is no point in keeping any
longer any of the white burgundies of the fifties. Whatever the
fate of the 1964s there is no need to drink them in 1966. The same
should be true of the finer German 1964s, but some of the lesser
Moselles will make excellent, young drinking. The 1964 Alsace
wines will be ready too, but are unlikely to outshine the 1961s.

Port-drinkers hardly need to be advised what to drink, but as
there is nothing between the light 1950s and the immature 1955s
(only one shipper declared 1954), the tendency to drink up the
very fine but powerful 1945s and the excellent 1948s will grow.
The 1947s are still useful but not great ports, without much
expectation of long life. Some of the late-bottled, and therefore
early maturing, ports, are well-worth considering, although
unpopular with traditionalists.

Although the champagne-shippers naturally advertise the
merits of their latest vintage, I believe that the last-but-one
often makes the better drinking. The 1953s were better than the
1955s when the latter were first introduced, and the 1955s better

than the succeeding 1959s. These in turn will be followed by the 1961s, which should be exceptionally good and may well be introduced in 1966. It is possible that the 1959s, owing to the prevalent lowness of acidity in that year, will not surpass their predecessors, nor last as well as some vintages. But champagne is, after all, a 'made' wine, and it is not difficult to improve the balance of a vintage champagne by the addition of a small amount of wine from more acid adjacent vintages. Nevertheless, I believe that vintage champagne does not have to be drunk too young; nor good non-vintage champagne for that matter. For bottle age gives additional flavour. Ten years old strikes me as an ideal age for champagne; by then it has lost some of its exuberant sparkle, and one can actually taste the wine—not, it must be admitted, the first consideration of many champagne-drinkers.

A neglected wine for drinking—though hardly worth adding to a regular buying list—is madeira. It is the most long-lived of all fortified wines. Not long ago, at a tasting of fine old madeiras, I sampled a 1910 Verdelho, which was vigorous and young in flavour, at an age when most vintage ports show definite signs of flagging. At this particular tasting I drank madeiras back to 1838. Since about 1890, vintage wines have nearly all been replaced by those made on the solera system, but they can still be excellent, and at a time when mature vintage port is both rare and expensive, madeira is a ready alternative to accompany dessert. But it must be old, and therefore fairly dear, for the cheaper madeiras lack much distinction; there must be that touch of nutty dryness at the end of even the richest bual or malmsey.

Another alternative for after-dinner drinking is old-bottled sherry, a favourite of earlier generations but almost killed by the last war. However they are reappearing here and there on wine merchants' lists. As all fine sherry blends include a proportion of old sherries, the long bottle-age needed for port or madeira is unnecessary. Relatively full wines benefit most from bottle age, and ten to fifteen years transforms a fine amontillado or oloroso; the flavour bears more than a passing resemblance to madeira. For those with storage space, it is worth considering putting away a few bottles of the fuller, finer sherries every year. They must be good to start with, but even three or four years in bottle makes an appreciable difference.

This programme, particularly on the buying side, may sound ambitious; buying usually seems more extravagant than consuming. But it is the pattern rather than the purchases that is significant, for few of us buy steadily through the wine list from port at one end to cognac at the other. The secret of buying vintage wines—and particularly the reds—is to purchase early and to keep. 'What we have we hold' is no bad motto for a wine-amateur's cellar, even if a merchant actually does much of the holding on his behalf. Wine-drinkers less wise in their generation, when confronted with fine bottles bought years earlier by their more prudent friends at prices that later seem extraordinarily low, sometimes imply that the latter have had unfair if enviable advantages. Yet the early buyers may well have spent less on better wines than those who buy from hand to mouth.

Few of us can buy all the wines we like, but most can buy systematically our favourite types; the rest can be added as and when possible. A claret-drinker who had bought and mainly kept say, ten varied dozen apiece of the twelve good vintages between 1945 and 1962, or a Burgundian who had acquired a similar variety of the ten good burgundy vintages in the same period, might well congratulate himself today; not perhaps a compleat but a contented imbiber.

Goat and Compasses

By etymologies of public houses
Many are tempted to rash speculation.
This 'Goat and Compasses', where now we tend,
Must surely have a likelier derivation
Than 'God encompasseth us'—such irony
Could any mind unprejudiced admit?
Step to the bar and order what you will,
And in our private angle as we sit
These compasses can signify the force
That holds our thoughts within the civil order;
The goat obscenely leads them in a dance
Up to the outlaw country on the border.
The anarchic goat and rational compasses,
These are the warring standards that divide:
But here in conference in our private angle
Under this sign our thoughts are pacified.

JAMES REEVES